# COOPERSTOWN
# DREAMS

A Week You Will Never Forget

Eric Walczykowski

The purpose of this book is to chronicle one team's
experience at Cooperstown Dreams Park through the eyes
of its coach.

Some of the names of the players in this book have been
changed to honor their privacy.

This book is also available in e-book format.

Walczykowski, Eric.
Cooperstown Dreams / by Eric Walczykowski

ISBN: 978-1-7347198-2-6


1.   Youth Sports  2. Baseball  3. Sports and Outdoors


Printed in the United States of America.

Photo credits to Colleen Walczykowski and Garrett Rea.

Box scores courtesy of GameChanger.

# DEDICATION

To my two boys, Devon and Jordan. Being with both of you on the baseball field at Cooperstown Dreams Park was truly a dream come true.

It has been a joy to watch you grow in the game of baseball, a path to growth in life.

This was one of the best weeks of my life and I hope you have the opportunity to experience something like this with your children.

# CONTENTS

# Special Thanks

To my wife, Colleen Walczykowski, for being an unwavering ally as I pursue dreams. Her support for the Cooperstown trip allowed me to have one of the best weeks of my life.

To the parents of the Hard 90 Clutch, thank you for affording me the opportunity to coach your boys. It has been an incredible journey, and I am truly honored to have been able to share time on the baseball field with such fine young men.

To the great athletes of the Hard 90 Clutch, thank you for your time and dedication to the game of baseball. I am blessed to have had the opportunity to coach each and every one of you. Keep working hard and you will accomplish all you seek in life!

# 1

## FOREWORD

Each year over 1,000 teams from all over North America make the pilgrimage to Cooperstown, baseball's birthplace.

These 12-and-under teams are in search of the magic of baseball—a magic that only the home of baseball can provide.

The stories of the Cooperstown experience are passed down like folklore. *"It's like Disneyland for baseball fans." "A week you'll never forget."*

The tales of the 12U legends live large. *"That kid looked like Verlander on the mound—he must have been up to 75." "Did you see how far he hit that ball? That was a moonshot. Probably 300 feet."*

These 12U teams are treated to a weeklong camp in which they get to sleep with their teammates and coaches in barrack-style dormitories.

For many, this trip is the longest time they have spent away from their parents. It is an unbelievably fun time and an experience to help them grow, becoming good young men.

The summer days in Cooperstown are spent playing baseball with teams from all over the U.S., some of which began when the boys were six. Other teams were assembled just for this tournament.

Some are Little League teams in search of a fun experience. Others are travel ball teams that have been training to win the Cooperstown championship.

The original park, Cooperstown Dreams Park, hosts 104 teams per week. This was the park that started it all in 1996. The idea was sparked with a simple comment made by a father and grandfather who loved baseball:

"Every kid in America should have the opportunity to play baseball in Cooperstown." —Lou Presutti, Sr.

A second park, Cooperstown All Star Village, was created in 1999. This park hosts upward of 60 teams a week.

Hard 90 Baseball has been sending teams to Cooperstown to play at both parks since 2006.

Going to Cooperstown with 12-15 youth baseball players is extremely rewarding. It's amazing to glimpse the history of baseball through the eyes of babes.

This experience far exceeds folklore and is worth every penny. It takes you back to simpler times, allowing kids to be kids by playing baseball all day and well into the night and by fostering Cooperstown dreams for a lifetime.

Here's a look at the Hard 90 Clutch—a band of brothers that made the pilgrimage to Cooperstown Dreams Park in 2019. This was a week I'll never forget!

# 2

## INTRODUCTION

There were no outs in the top of the first inning of pool-play game number 4. The Hard 90 Clutch found themselves down 5-0 to a stacked Copperheads team from South Carolina.

The two undefeated powerhouse clubs were squaring off in a game that was sure to decide the winner of the bracket in the six-game pool-play format. The winner of the bracket would earn a top-10 seed and several important byes in the 104-team tournament on a quest to win the championship.

Both teams sent top pitchers to the mound. The Hard 90 Clutch had Ryan on the hill—an ace pitcher who had won several big bracket-play games for the Clutch over the last several years. With Ryan on the mound the team played with confidence. He's not overpowering, but he commands three pitches—fastball, changeup, breaking ball—that keep opposing hitters off balance.

On this steamy, overcast morning in Cooperstown, the Copperheads had Ryan's number. The first batter sent an 0-2 fastball over the right field fence for a home run. Two batters later, their stout number-three hitter destroyed an 0-1 breaking ball over the center-field fence.

Then the Copperheads' cleanup hitter laced a 3-1 changeup to left field for the third hard-hit ball of the game. The Clutch was now down 3-0 with no outs.

The Hard 90 coaches conferred and with a deep pitching staff and the need for a momentum shift, Jordan was brought in to pitch. Jordan is the only 11-year-old on the Clutch, a wiry lefty who can reach the mid-to-upper 60s with a nasty breaking ball.

Jordan struck out the fifth batter—but he reached on the dropped third strike, which also allowed the cleanup hitter to advance to third.

Leading 3-0 with runners on first and third and no outs, the Copperheads stole second base. Sensing that every run would matter in this game, the Copperheads coach called for a suicide squeeze— a play where the runner breaks for the plate while the batter lays down a bunt.

In this particular case, the batter missed the bunt, but the play caught Hard 90's sure-handed catcher by surprise. His throw to try to nail the runner scampering back to third was wild, allowing two more runs to score. Copperheads 5, Hard 90 0.

Jordan was able to get out of the inning with a pickoff, another strikeout, and a ground ball to shortstop. The Hard 90 Clutch, a usually upbeat team, came to the dugout dejected, trailing 5-0 in what was sure to be a dog fight.

After a quick team meeting where the coaches reminded the players that they were in a field with shorter-than-usual outfield dimensions, the Clutch was not out of the fight.

The Copperheads sent their ace to the hill: a fire-balling right hander who looked to have a fastball of 75 mph and a filthy breaking ball. He wasted no time recording three outs, and the Hard 90 Clutch found themselves back in the field, chasing five runs.

Was this poor start going to derail the Clutch's Cooperstown dreams? You can never count out this scrappy team. But more on that later.

# 3

## THE CLUTCH BEGINS

The idea for the Hard 90 Clutch was birthed on a foggy morning in Cooperstown back in August 2015. The Hard 90 Legacy Premier was wrapping up its Cooperstown run on Championship Thursday.

Eric was the assistant coach for his son Devon's team. The boys on the Legacy Premier had been together for about three years. Some had been playing together since they were seven.

While these boys were good friends going into Cooperstown, the weeklong experience at Cooperstown Dreams Park only brought them even closer together.

The boys were inseparable during the week, playing Wiffle ball, heading over to the snack shack, pin trading, making limited-edition pins with Sharpies, and of course playing baseball.

The Legacy Premier was a stacked team that played well together. Unfortunately, a lapse of focus in pool play led them to a tough loss against the 83rd-ranked team, which dropped them from the seventh seed to the 22nd seed.

This pool-play loss set up a Wednesday-night playoff game with the ninth seed from Florida. The tough Florida team was shocked to see the Legacy Premier on Wednesday night.

In the top of the first, six of the first seven Legacy Premier hitters homered. The one who didn't hit a double off the top of the wall.

Down 7-0, the Florida team brought in their ace to pitch and it was a back-and-forth battle with Legacy Premier prevailing, 11-10.

Unfortunately, with the emotionally draining game on Wednesday night, Legacy Premier could not answer the bell on Thursday morning and lost to a tough California team, 6-1, in a lackluster performance.

While the early loss on Championship Thursday was disappointing, the overall experience was absolutely amazing. Coach Eric really enjoyed seeing good buddies bond over a weeklong baseball summer camp experience.

Coach Eric wanted his younger son Jordan to have the same experience, but this time he wanted both of his boys to join him in the barracks. It was then that the idea for the Clutch was born.

Hard 90 Clutch target date: July 2019 in Cooperstown.

# 4

## THE CLUTCH OVER THE YEARS

The Hard 90 Clutch officially formed as the Hard 90 Pound Premier in the spring of 2015. The team was registered as an 8U team, but they played 9U, because there were no 8U tournaments in Northern California.

Jordan, Brady, and Ben were the original Clutch players who started with the Pound Premier in the inaugural season. New to travel baseball, the boys worked hard and learned the new, faster pace of travel baseball.

After the inaugural 8U season, the team held a summer tryout and added three more Clutch players: Jack, Eric and Ryan. With a team nucleus forming, the 9U season was an aggressive campaign. The Hard 90 philosophy is to play the very best competition.

The team sought out this competition throughout Northern California, Southern California, and Arizona. These battles, both triumphs and defeats, prepared the boys to stay calm under pressure and taught them the valuable lesson that you are never out of the fight.

In fall of 2016, the Clutch added Ty and Ian to the team's strong nucleus, making this last season of the Pound phenomenal. In the final tournament, the Pound won the championship in the California Fall State Classic, a tournament that featured some of the top teams in California.

The following fall, the Clutch was born. In the open tryout, Scott and Carter were added to round out the team.

With 10 of the 11 players who would make up the Cooperstown Clutch, work began on getting them ready for the famous tournament that was two short years away.

A high-level Cooperstown meeting was held with the boys in the fall of 2017. Coach Eric spoke to them about Cooperstown, how much fun the trip would be, and that if they challenged themselves they could make a pretty deep run in the National Tournament with 104 teams.

During the 2017-18 season, the Clutch continued to take on all comers in Northern California, Southern California, Arizona, and Nevada. With the hotbed of baseball in

Northern California, the Clutch developed a few friendly rivalries that pushed the team to the limit each week.

At the end of that season, the Clutch hosted a tryout and added Taylor to complete the Cooperstown roster.

Let's meet the players:

Jordan, a wiry left-handed outfielder and pitcher, is a tenacious player. His older brother Devon played for Hard 90 and attended Cooperstown in 2015. Jordan is a whole year younger than the rest of the Clutch but has had some pretty big moments for the team, hitting two walk-off grand slams.

Brady, a tall right-handed pitcher and utility player, is one of the team leaders. He established himself as one of the most consistent pitchers and fierce competitors. He is a serious competitor and hard worker who is always willing to help push others to do their best.

Ben, a right-handed pitcher and outfielder, is the ace of the pitching staff. A consistent leadoff hitter, he is a quiet competitor who also has a low handicap on the links. Ben also is the resident linguist, helping translate big words used by the coaching staff to the rest of the team.

Jack, nicknamed "Captain," is a leader on the field with his steady defensive play at shortstop and ferocious hacks at the plate. This stout right-handed batter makes his presence known. His older brother also visited Cooperstown with Hard 90 in 2017, and Captain has had his eye on hitting more home runs than his older brother since his return.

Eric, a tall right-handed first baseman and pitcher, is always steady on the bump. The gentle giant is an outstanding teammate and helps out at catcher, too. Always willing to lend a helping hand, Eric is someone you can count on to give his best effort in big situations.

Ryan, a right-handed pitcher and utility player, is a big-game pitcher. He throws three pitches for strikes with a funky delivery that keeps teams off-balance. Ryan is also quick to make a teammate laugh. With an older brother who visited Cooperstown in 2016 with Hard 90, he is a fierce competitor who is never shaken under pressure.

Ty, a right-handed middle infielder, is the heart-and-soul of the team. He is always quick to pick up a teammate with words of encouragement. A serious competitor, Ty has been brought in to pitch in some big jams and has gotten the team out of the situations with a bulldog's tenacity.

Ian, a right-handed outfielder, is a relentless competitor. Off the field, Ian is good for a laugh, but on the field, he's all business. He really enjoys the game, his teammates, and fierce competition. When not on the baseball field, you can find Ian fishing the local rivers, lakes and ponds looking to hook his next bass.

Scott, a right-handed catcher, is a serious competitor. Although he has a great sense of humor, game time is serious business for Scott. He is team leader behind the dish and a favorite for Clutch pitchers to throw to. Rumor has it that he is also a ferocious soccer player.

Carter, a happy-go-lucky right-handed pitcher, infielder, and catcher, always has a smile on his face. He is a middle-of-the-order force for the Clutch and has pitched a number of big games. Always cool under pressure, Carter has had some big hits for the Clutch.

Taylor is a right-handed power player for the Clutch. A quiet but serious competitor, he shows big power at the plate and on the mound. Taylor is another Clutch player who does not crack under pressure.

Coach Devon is a right-handed first baseman at Jesuit High School and is committed to attend Pepperdine University on a baseball scholarship. He visited

Cooperstown Dreams Park with the Hard 90 Legacy Premier in 2015. A former catcher, he is an expert pitch caller who gets along great with the players.

Coach Garret has been the assistant coach of the Clutch since the forming of the original team at 8U. He coaches first base, works with the pitchers, and always has a positive word of encouragement for the boys.

Coach Eric is the owner of Hard 90 Baseball and has worked with the Hard 90 Clutch off and on since the forming of the original team. He took over the team as the manager at the beginning of the 12U season to prepare the team for the Cooperstown tournament.

# 5

## COOPERSTOWN FORMATION MEETING

With the roster complete, the Hard 90 coaches organized a team meeting in August 2018. The 11 boys sat in the Hard 90 gym in front of a whiteboard, discussing and debating the goals for the season.

After an hour of this, the Clutch boys presented a stated goal to win the 2019 Cooperstown Dreams Park tournament. They decided that in order to achieve that goal, they would each need to train for five or six days a week. Additionally, they wanted to play a schedule of the top competition in the Western United States to prepare themselves for whatever competition they met in Cooperstown.

Thus, the Hard 90 Clutch officially began their quest for Cooperstown. The boys worked out incessantly at the Hard 90 Clubhouse nearly every day for two to three hours. Many joined the Hard 90 Strive program, a thrice-per-week workout regimen that includes power throwing, power hitting, and strength and conditioning. This program was specifically designed to improve throwing velocity, batted-ball exit speed, and athleticism on the field.

In addition to Strive, the Clutch boys attended an outdoor and an indoor team practice each week. They kept their goals top of mind and held each other accountable to get their training in. The team also participated in two mental-game seminars: one called The Young Champion's Mind by Jim Afremow, the other called The Hard 90 Mindset by Hard 90 Owner Eric Walczykowski.

The boys played a rigorous tournament schedule that included all of the top 12U teams in Northern California. They also traveled to Las Vegas and Southern California to make sure that they got a chance to see all of the top teams in the Western United States.

During this tournament tour, the Clutch boys saw some of the very best pitching arms in the 12U division. In one tournament alone, they saw three pitchers that had fastballs of between 74 and 79 miles per hour.

While the team earned a .500 record during the tournament season and only won a handful of tournaments, the level of competition ensured that they would be ready for Cooperstown.

# 6

## Cooperstown Day 1

Most of the Hard 90 Clutch players had been waiting four to five years for the big first day at Cooperstown Dreams Park. Three of the Hard 90 Clutch players had older brothers visit Cooperstown with Hard 90 previously and had been waiting for their time to shine.

Coach Eric visited Cooperstown Dreams Park with his older son Devon on the Legacy Premier and could not wait for Jordan to be able to experience Cooperstown with his older brother as a coach. Coach Eric was excited to spend a week in the Disneyland of Baseball with his two boys and to coach Jordan with his best buddies.

The travel to Cooperstown from Sacramento, California makes for a long day, but the anticipation of reuniting with teammates for a weeklong summer baseball camp makes the time go by quickly.

The drive from the Syracuse or Albany airport to Cooperstown is gorgeous. It feels as if you are traveling back in time. Old houses, small towns, family farms, lakes, beautiful hills, and greenery line the roads. Heading down Highway 28 and driving up on Cooperstown Dreams Park is when the magic really begins.

Seemingly out of nowhere appear well-manicured grounds, with a grand entrance welcoming all 104 teams (approximately 1,250 12-year-olds, over 200 coaches and over 100 umpires.) The staff is a well-oiled machine and that welcomes you to their home and ushers you straight into the Village, which consists of over 100 barracks-style buildings the boys will call home for the next week.

The first impression of Cooperstown Dreams Park reminds you of the great dialogue from *Field of Dreams*:

**John Kinsella**: Is this heaven?

**Ray Kinsella:** It's Iowa.

**John Kinsella:** Iowa? I could have sworn this was heaven.

**John Kinsella:** Oh yeah. It's the place where dreams come true.

**Ray Kinsella:** [Ray looks around, seeing his wife playing with their daughter on the porch] Maybe this is heaven.

For all intents and purposes, the Cooperstown Dreams Park is the 12U Field of Dreams.

The Clutch arrived at Cooperstown around 9:00 p.m. Security is tight in the Village to ensure that all is safe for the 12U campers. The Clutch boys would be spending the next week in a barrack-style dormitory with eight bunk beds that would house the 11 Clutch players and three coaches.

The Clutch parents began arranging the barracks just right for the boys to spend the next week. This included making up beds, installing extension cords, and setting up fans, among other things.

All the while, the boys were waiting patiently for their parents to head back to their houses so they could hang out with their buddies. Shortly after the parents left, the boys had some free time to catch up and head over to the snack shack to enjoy a hamburger, hot dog, or some candy.

During their free time, some of the boys made quick work of pin trading. Almost all of the 104 teams bring with them a pin commemorating the trip and symbolizing their organization and hometown. Additionally, some of the employees and umpires make special pins to share with the boys as well. Pin trading is the underground commerce of Cooperstown Dreams Park and the boys have a ton of fun with it.

At 10:00 p.m, the Clutch started their first of what would be nightly meetings. The agenda was to lay the ground rules for the week and to discuss expectations and the daily schedule.

After the 15-minute meeting, the boys were off to the restrooms to brush their teeth and get ready for bed.

At 10:30 p.m., it was lights out for the boys—even if some fell asleep closer to midnight due to the excitement. Some whispering, giggling, and even some farting may have taken place.

The day finally arrived! The Hard 90 Clutch was in Cooperstown for the week of their lives.

# 7

## COOPERSTOWN DAY 2

Day 2 started at 7:00 a.m., the official wake-up time for the Hard 90 Clutch. The team discussed the importance of waking up at the same time every day to get on a routine. Each player made their bed and headed for the showers to start their day off right.

The first morning in the barracks, every player on the Hard 90 Clutch popped right out of bed. There was so much excitement and anticipation of what they might find and do at Cooperstown Dreams Park.

Coach Garrett (the resident DJ) got the tunes going on the Bluetooth speaker early and often for the Clutch boys. He was always ready to take a request from a player for their favorite song.

The team ate breakfast together at 8:00 a.m. in the cafeteria before each player was checked out of the facility by their parents to head into downtown Cooperstown. Day 2 was the first official day of the MLB Hall of Fame Induction Ceremonies and the team headed into town to meet up with some Hall of Famers.

Downtown, the Hard 90 Clutch had the opportunity to meet a number of big leaguers including Pete Rose, Andre Dawson, Jesse Barfield, and Denny McLain, among others. The downtown was buzzing, as this was a big induction year for one of the home-state teams: Mariano Rivera from the New York Yankees was the first unanimous selection for the Hall of Fame.

The boys had a ton of fun checking out the Hall of Famers and all of the baseball shops on Main Street. The national hit is the Baseballism store, but there are a ton of other memorabilia stores and bat companies to check out. Many of the boys met up at Sal's Pizzeria of Cooperstown for a slice of their legendary pie.

Hall of Fame Induction weekend creates a carnival buzz in Cooperstown that only happens once a year. Everyone was talking about Mariano Rivera, perhaps the best closer of all time.

Captain Jack and Coach Devon— the two Clutch Yankees fans—were in heaven. They did not mind the constant teasing from the rest of the team—after all, they were in Cooperstown when one of their heroes would be enshrined in the Hall of Fame!

Other 2019 Hall of Fame inductees included Roy Halladay, Harold Baines, Edgar Martinez, Mike Mussina, and Lee Smith.

The team checked back into the facility at 1:00 p.m. to begin Opening Day ceremonies. The boys were fired up from the experience of downtown Cooperstown. They were sharing stories and showing autographs and memorabilia they purchased while in town.

The Clutch met to review the schedule for the rest of the day, which included a number of Cooperstown Dreams Park organizational meetings, Opening Ceremonies, and the Skills Competition.

At the meeting, the boys also discussed the Skills Competition participants. They were asked who wanted to participate in each individual skills event, and as anticipated, every player volunteered.

The coaches discussed the importance of the value of meritocracy at Hard 90 Baseball (yes, our resident linguistic expert Ben helped us all with the definition of meritocracy).

The coaches then asked the players which stat from the season most represented the skills. It was decided that home runs represented the Home Run Derby, pitch command represented the Golden Arm, and steals represented the Road Runner.

So for the Hard 90 Clutch, Jordan would be participating in the Home Run Derby, Ben would be throwing in the Golden Arm Competition, and Brady would be running in the Road Runner race.

After the meeting, the team donned their blue "away" uniforms for the very first time to attend the festivities.

The procession kicked off with an all-camp meeting at the cafeteria where the Cooperstown Dreams Park team discussed the ground rules for the week, including an important talk on respecting the baseball uniform and the great game of baseball. A key point that the chief operating officer of Cooperstown Dreams Park made is that a uniform and the game is what you make of it. If you respect the uniform and the game, each will continue to hold a position of value.

In addition to the uniform talk, players were instructed on how to properly wear a baseball uniform. This instruction included a warning of a game suspension if the uniform rules were violated.

Players were also treated to a bit of history on Cooperstown Dreams Park: the reason for its founding, how it has grown over the years, and some home-run records.

After the 2:00 p.m. meeting, the Hard 90 Clutch headed to the photography studio for individual and team pictures. Afterward, the team grabbed a quick bite at the cafeteria before reporting for the Opening Ceremony Parade.

The Hard 90 Clutch reported to the cafeteria tent for the Opening Ceremony Parade. It was extremely hot sitting in the tent (as upstate New York summers can be). Still, the anticipation of the Opening Ceremony made the blistering heat bearable.

All 104 teams were present, and the boys were anxious to get the parade going. Everyone was hooting, hollering, and banging on the fold-up tables—the kids could not contain their excitement.

And just like that, the parade started. The announcer started calling out teams one by one. The PA Announcer called "Hard 90 Clutch" from the bullhorn and the team was off—Cooperstown week had started.

The team marched three by three into Little Majors Stadium, which is the showpiece of Cooperstown Dreams Park. Only the championship game is played there each week, and it was packed for Opening Ceremonies. Every fan for every team was in the stands, cheering for their players as loud as they could!

Once again, the announcer shouted out "Hard 90 Clutch," and the boys proudly marched into Little Majors Stadium to thunderous applause from their families seated down the right-field line. Each parent held a giant player-head cutout on a stick. It was an amazing welcome from the Clutch's #1 fans.

At the end of the march, the Clutch took their spot in left field to view the festivities. The team was treated to dances by two Hawaiian teams, including the famous Maori dance the Haka; the Canadian National Anthem sung by the Canadian Team; and the Star-Spangled Banner sung by a parent from one of the U.S. teams. Everywhere you looked you saw flags and smiling faces. The highlight of the ceremony was a reading of the poem "I Am Your Flag" and a tribute to the fallen soldiers who played at Cooperstown Dreams Park.

After the ceremony, the players were released to the individual skills competitions. The highlight of the skills competition was Around the Horn, where the Clutch took eighth place out of 104 teams, missing the top six (and finals round) by a very small margin.

At the closing of the ceremony, the Clutch headed back to the barracks for some free time before the 10:00 p.m. meeting. At the meeting, the boys reflected on three things that stood out during their day. The first was spending time with their teammates in Cooperstown, followed by the opportunity to speak to MLB players and get some advice from them. By far the best advice was from Denny McLain: Keep the ball down and study hard in school!

After each player texted his three favorite things from that day to his parents, they met with their daily buddy to discuss what they needed to do to be successful in the tournament. The team reconvened to share with the entire team their individual keys to success that they entered into their phone for review in the morning.

At 10:30, the Clutch went to sleep, a successful Day 2 in the books.

# 8

## COOPERSTOWN DAY 3

Game day was finally here!

The boys woke up at 7:00 a.m., the mandatory wake-up time for the Hard 90 Clutch. Little did they know, getting up at the same time every day would help them later on in the tournament.

After waking up, the boys made their beds and showered before a brief morning meeting to preview the day. They then headed to the cafeteria for breakfast.

Next, they headed over to the practice area for a morning workout. The team ran through pick sequences before taking some batting practice. They then met behind the cages to watch other teams take their cuts.

After reviewing about 20 opposing players, the team determined that only two out of 20 were swinging "with intent to do damage." The coaches discussed the need to make every swing count. Make the decision to swing with intent before you get in the box, and simplify the decision process to only one decision: to not swing.

The boys grabbed some lunch before meeting briefly to review the objectives for the 1:45 game. Game 1 featured a matchup with the Fury, a tough team from Downers Grove, Illinois. Donning their red uniforms, the Hard 90 Clutch would be the home team, sending Carter to the mound.

The boys had some butterflies heading out, but those quickly went away as Carter shut the Fury down in the first inning. Two lineouts, a groundout, and it was the Clutch's turn to bat.

In their half of the first, the Clutch took command, putting up eight runs, all scored with two outs. Captain Jack led the game off with a hard-hit single and the hit parade began. Ty, batting eighth, got the Clutch home run party started by sending a fastball over the left-center-field fence. Two batters later Captain Jack was back up to bat, hitting his first home run of the tournament, a no-doubter way over the center-field fence. One inning played: Hard 90 Clutch 8, Downers Grove 0.

Carter was lights-out on the mound, supported by stellar defense. Taylor also returned to the hill for the first time in four months, tossing two scoreless frames. Ty, Jack, and Taylor all homered for the Clutch.

In game 1, the team learned the importance of respecting the game and their opponent. Leading by 10 runs, the Clutch shut down the offensive attack entirely by not stealing bases or advancing on passed balls and wild pitches.

The final score of the game was 15-5. The team then headed over to Maskot's, a pizza parlor across the street from Cooperstown Dreams Park, for a quick meal between games. It was a magical sight to see the boys eating together and talking about the game.

After a late lunch, the team returned to the barracks to prepare for game 2 with the Central Florida Pride, a tough team with sights on winning the entire tournament.

Florida had its ace on the mound, and he was going to be a tough match for the Clutch; his fastball was in the low 70s and he had a sharp-breaking hammer. He shut the Clutch down in the first, and the Florida team jumped out to a quick two-run lead in their half against Clutch ace, Ben.

The game then settled down and two ace pitchers served up out after out until the fifth inning, when Florida scored two more runs to take what seemed to be a commanding 4-0 lead into the top of the sixth and final inning.

The Hard 90 Clutch team had never been afraid of a deficit, coming from behind several times that year to swipe a victory from the jaws of defeat. One of the beauties of baseball is that you always get your turn—a team can't run out the clock. The Clutch was focused—this was the third time through the order for many of the boys.

The inning started off with a walk and a strikeout. An error by the pitcher (a sure double-play ball) set the stage for Brady to get the Clutch party started. On the very first pitch he saw, Brady put the ball way over the right center field fence for a three-run bomb. The game was now 4-3 in favor of the Florida team.

After another strikeout, the Clutch sent Eric Erdmann to the plate for his first at-bat of the game. After swinging and missing at the first pitch, Eric hit a rocket to the right center field fence for a single, keeping the Clutch's chances alive.

Next up was Ryan, who advanced to first on a dropped third strike, setting the stage for Captain Jack. On the first pitch, Jack was ready to go: he took a vicious hack that just missed under the ball (wow—the whole team envisioned the game-changing home run that could have been). After taking the next pitch for a ball, there was that vicious swing again, but this time he connected for a three-run home run to give the Clutch their first lead of the game, 6-4!

The Clutch boys went crazy, pouring out of the dugout to meet the Captain at home plate.

After Jack's home run, Jordan and Ben hit back-to-back home runs, making three dingers in a row for the Clutch. The Clutch put up three more runs to take an 11-4 lead into the bottom of the sixth.

But the Florida team was not going away. It scored five runs before bringing the tying run to the plate with two outs. Captain Jack served up a fastball that was hit deep to right field. It went way back, but Clutch right fielder Brady had just enough room at the fence to make the final out. The Clutch prevailed, 11-9.

The boys were fired up to escape this tough battle with a win. The Clutch started a new tradition after winning the game by running down the right field line to high-five all the fans in the spectators box.

This was to be just the first of the emotional comebacks for the Clutch. The game home runs by Brady, Jack, Jordan, and Ben, bringing the day's total to seven for the team.

After saying good-night to their parents, the club headed back to the barracks for their postgame meeting, where the boys individually and collectively reflected on their gratitude for the day. Without a doubt, the team was thankful for time with teammates, two wins, a handful of home runs, and some bonding time at Maskot's.

What a day for the Clutch: 2-0 heading into Day 4.

| | 1 | 2 | 3 | 4 | 5 | 6 | R | H | E |
|---|---|---|---|---|---|---|---|---|---|
| DWNR | 0 | 0 | 3 | 2 | 0 | 0 | 5 | 5 | 4 |
| CLTC | 6 | 5 | 2 | 0 | 0 | X | 15 | 14 | 3 |

## 5 Downers Grove Fury Black 12U

Sunday, July 21
10:45AM

## Hard 90 Clutch 12U 15

### Downers Grove Fury Black 12U more stats

| Lineup | AB | R | H | RBI | BB | SO |
|---|---|---|---|---|---|---|
| Owen C. | 3 | 1 | 1 | 1 | 0 | 0 |
| Brody S. | 3 | 0 | 2 | 0 | 0 | 1 |
| Ramzi T. | 3 | 0 | 0 | 0 | 0 | 0 |
| Adam M. | 1 | 1 | 0 | 0 | 1 | 0 |
| Hank A. | 3 | 0 | 0 | 0 | 0 | 1 |
| Dominic W. | 2 | 1 | 0 | 0 | 0 | 0 |
| Will R. | 3 | 0 | 1 | 1 | 0 | 0 |
| John M. | 1 | 1 | 0 | 0 | 1 | 1 |
| James B. | 2 | 0 | 0 | 0 | 0 | 1 |
| Ryan G. | 2 | 0 | 0 | 0 | 0 | 0 |
| Jace M. | 2 | 1 | 1 | 0 | 0 | 0 |
| Totals | 25 | 5 | 5 | 2 | 2 | 4 |

**Batting**
TB: Owen C., Jace M., Will R., Brody S. 2
RBI: Owen C., Will R.
ROE: Ryan G., Ramzi T., Dominic W.
HBP: Dominic W.
GIDP: Will R.
SB: Owen C., Ryan G., Adam M., Brody S., Dominic W.

Totals
Team QAB: 7 (25.00%)
Owen C., Ryan G., John M., Adam M., Brody S. 2, Ramzi T.

Team LOB: 5

### Clutch more stats

| Lineup | AB | R | H | RBI | BB | SO |
|---|---|---|---|---|---|---|
| Jack S. | 4 | 2 | 2 | 2 | 0 | 0 |
| Jordan W. | 4 | 0 | 0 | 0 | 0 | 2 |
| Ben R. | 4 | 2 | 2 | 0 | 0 | 0 |
| Carter G. | 3 | 0 | 2 | 0 | 1 | 0 |
| Brady R. | 4 | 3 | 1 | 3 | 0 | 0 |
| | 1 | 1 | 0 | 1 | 0 | 0 |
| Taylor S. | 2 | 2 | 2 | 3 | 0 | 0 |
| Ian P. | 3 | 1 | 1 | 1 | 0 | 0 |
| Ty M. | 2 | 1 | 2 | 1 | 0 | 0 |
| Ryan T. | 1 | 1 | 0 | 0 | 0 | 0 |
| Eric E. | 2 | 0 | 1 | 0 | 0 | 1 |
| Scott B. | 1 | 2 | 1 | 0 | 0 | 0 |
| Totals | 31 | 15 | 14 | 11 | 1 | 3 |

**Batting**
2B: Brady R.
HR: Ty M., Jack S., Taylor S.
TB: Scott B., Eric E., Carter G. 2, Ty M. 5, Ian P., Ben R. 2, Brady R. 2, Jack S. 5, Taylor S. 3
RBI: Ty M., Ian P., Brady R. 3, Jack S. 2, Taylor S. 3, Ryan T.
ROE: Brady R., Cade T.
FC: Brady R.
SB: Ben R.

Totals
Team QAB: 14 (43.75%)
Carter G. 4, Ty M. 2, Ian P., Ben R., Brady R., Jack S. 2, Taylor S. 2, Jordan W.

Team LOB: 2

Fielding
E: Ryan T., Jack S., Taylor S.
DP: Brady R., Jack S., Taylor S.

### Downers Grove Fury Black 12U more stats

| Pitching | IP | #P | S% | H | R | ER | SO | BB | HR |
|---|---|---|---|---|---|---|---|---|---|
| Ramzi T. | 1.0 | 33 | .636 | 5 | 8 | 0 | 1 | 1 | 2 |
| Adam M. | 1.0 | 34 | .618 | 6 | 5 | 3 | 2 | 0 | 0 |
| Will R. | 3.0 | 29 | .621 | 3 | 2 | 2 | 0 | 0 | 1 |
| Totals | 5.0 | 96 | .625 | 14 | 15 | 5 | 3 | 1 | 3 |

Pitching
L: Ramzi T.
WP: Adam M., Ramzi T.
Pitches-Strikes: Adam M. 34-21, Will R. 29-18, Ramzi T. 33-21
Groundouts-Flyouts: Adam M. 0-1, Will R. 2-6, Ramzi T. 2-0
First pitch strikes-Batters faced: Adam M. 5-9, Will R. 7-12, Ramzi T. 7-11

### Clutch more stats

| Pitching | IP | #P | S% | H | R | ER | SO | BB | HR |
|---|---|---|---|---|---|---|---|---|---|
| Carter G. | 4.0 | 73 | .571 | 4 | 5 | 2 | 3 | 2 | 0 |
| Taylor S. | 2.0 | 21 | .714 | 1 | 0 | 0 | 1 | 0 | 0 |
| Totals | 6.0 | 91 | .604 | 5 | 5 | 2 | 4 | 2 | 0 |

Pitching
W: Carter G.
HBP: Carter G.
WP: Carter G. 3
Pitches-Strikes: Carter G. 70-40, Taylor S. 21-15
Groundouts-Flyouts: Carter G. 6-3, Taylor S. 4-0
First pitch strikes-Batters faced: Carter G. 9-21, Taylor S. 5-7

# Hard 90 Clutch 12U Defeats Downers Grove Fury Black 12U Despite Allowing 3-Run Inning

Despite allowing three runs in the third inning, Hard 90 Clutch 12U defeated Downers Grove Fury Black 12U 15-5 on Sunday. The big inning for Downers Grove Fury Black 12U came thanks to a single by Owen C and an error on a ball put in play by Ramzi T.

Hard 90 Clutch 12U secured the victory thanks to eight runs in the first inning. Brady R, Ian P, Ty M, and Jack S each had RBIs in the frame.

Hard 90 Clutch 12U opened up scoring in the first inning, when an error scored two runs for Hard 90 Clutch 12U.

Carter G earned the win for Hard 90 Clutch 12U. He lasted four innings, allowing four hits and five runs while striking out three. Taylor S threw two innings in relief out of the bullpen.

Ramzi took the loss for Downers Grove Fury Black 12U. He lasted one inning, allowing five hits and eight runs while striking out one and walking one.

Hard 90 Clutch 12U smacked three home runs on the day. Jack had a long ball in the first inning. Taylor had a four bagger in the third inning. Ty went yard in the first inning.

Hard 90 Clutch 12U racked up 14 hits in the game. Ben R, Ty, Carter, Jack, and Taylor each collected multiple hits for Hard 90 Clutch 12U. Taylor, Jack, Carter, Ty, and Ben each collected two hits to lead Hard 90 Clutch 12U.

Brody S went 2-for-3 at the plate to lead Downers Grove Fury Black 12U in hits.

| | 1 | 2 | 3 | 4 | 5 | 6 | R | H | E |
|---|---|---|---|---|---|---|---|---|---|
| CLTC | 0 | 0 | 0 | 0 | 0 | 11 | 11 | 13 | 2 |
| 015C | 2 | 0 | 0 | 0 | 2 | 5 | 9 | 11 | 5 |

Final   League Game   Cooperstown Dreams Park, Cooperstown, NY, USA

**11** Hard 90 Clutch 12U

Sunday, July 21
4:00PM

**015 Central Florida Pride 12U** **9**

| Lineup | AB | R | H | RBI | BB | SO | Lineup | AB | R | H | RBI | BB | SO |
|---|---|---|---|---|---|---|---|---|---|---|---|---|---|
| Jack S. | 4 | 1 | 3 | 3 | 0 | 0 | Player 15-9 | 4 | 2 | 2 | 0 | 0 | 0 |
| Jordan W. | 4 | 1 | 1 | 1 | 0 | 2 | Player 15-10 | 3 | 2 | 3 | 0 | 0 | 0 |
| Ben R. | 3 | 1 | 1 | 1 | 1 | 0 | Player 15-15 | 3 | 1 | 1 | 2 | 0 | 0 |
| Carter G. | 4 | 1 | 1 | 0 | 0 | 2 | Player 15-12 | 3 | 1 | 2 | 1 | 0 | 0 |
| Taylor S. | 3 | 2 | 0 | 0 | 1 | 1 | Player 15-4 | 3 | 1 | 1 | 4 | 0 | 1 |
| Brady R. | 4 | 2 | 4 | 5 | 0 | 0 | Player 15-1 | 1 | 1 | 0 | 0 | 1 | 0 |
| Scott B. | 4 | 0 | 1 | 0 | 0 | 2 | Player 15-14 | 3 | 0 | 0 | 0 | 0 | 0 |
| Ty M. | 2 | 2 | 1 | 1 | 0 | 0 | Player 15-3 | 3 | 0 | 0 | 0 | 0 | 0 |
| Ian P. | 1 | 0 | 0 | 0 | 0 | 1 | Player 15-8 | 3 | 1 | 1 | 2 | 0 | 0 |
| Eric E. | 1 | 0 | 1 | 0 | 0 | 0 | Player 15-13 | 1 | 0 | 0 | 0 | 0 | 0 |
| Ryan T. | 3 | 1 | 0 | 0 | 0 | 2 | Player 15-11 | 1 | 0 | 1 | 0 | 0 | 0 |
| | | | | | | | Player 15-2 | 1 | 0 | 0 | 0 | 0 | 1 |
| Totals | 33 | 11 | 13 | 11 | 2 | 10 | Totals | 29 | 9 | 11 | 9 | 1 | 2 |

Batting
**HR:** Ben R., Brady R., Jack S., Jordan W.
**TB:** Scott B., Eric E., Carter G., Ty M., Ben R. 4, Brady R. 7, Jack S. 3, Jordan W. 4
**RBI:** Ty M., Ben R., Brady R. 5, Jack S. 3, Jordan W.
**ROE:** Scott B., Carter G., Taylor S.
**GIDP:** Ty M.
**SB:** Taylor S.
**CS:** Brady R.

Totals
**Team QAB:** 18 (45.71%)
Scott B., Eric E., Ty M., Ian P., Ben R. 3, Brady R. 3, Ryan T., Jack S. 2, Taylor S. 2, Jordan W.

**Team LOB:** 6

Fielding
**E:** Carter G., Jack S.
**DP:** Jack S., Taylor S.

Batting
**HR:** Player 15-4, Player 15-8
**Grand slam:** Player 15-4
**TB:** Player 16-4 4, Player 15-8 4, Player 15-9 2, Player 15-10 3, Player 15-11, Player 15-12 2, Player 15-15
**RBI:** Player 15-4 4, Player 15-8 2, Player 15-12, Player 15-15 2
**ROE:** Player 15-8, Player 15-15
**FC:** Player 15-14, Player 15-15
**HBP:** Player 15-1, Player 15-13
**GIDP:** Player 15-4
**SB:** Player 15-8, Player 15-10 2
**PIK:** Player 15-15

Totals
**Team QAB:** 7 (21.68%)
Player 15-1, Player 15-4, Player 15-8, Player 15-9, Player 15-10 2, Player 15-12

**Team LOB:** 5

Fielding
**E:** Player 15-1, Player 15-10, Player 15-12, Player 15-15
**DP:** Player 15-3, Player 15-9

Clutch more stats

015 Central Florida Pride 12U more stats

| Pitching | IP | #P | S% | H | R | ER | SO | BB | HR |
|---|---|---|---|---|---|---|---|---|---|
| Ben R. | 5.0 | 66 | .712 | 10 | 8 | 7 | 2 | 0 | 1 |
| Jack S. | 1.0 | 21 | .524 | 1 | 1 | 1 | 0 | 1 | 1 |
| Totals | 6.0 | 87 | .667 | 11 | 9 | 8 | 2 | 1 | 2 |

| Pitching | IP | #P | S% | H | R | ER | SO | BB | HR |
|---|---|---|---|---|---|---|---|---|---|
| Player 15-12 | 5.2 | 90 | .789 | 11 | 8 | 2 | 9 | 1 | 4 |
| Player 15-15 | 0.1 | 21 | .476 | 2 | 3 | 2 | 1 | 1 | 0 |
| Totals | 6.0 | 111 | .730 | 13 | 11 | 2 | 10 | 2 | 4 |

Pitching
**W:** Ben R.
**SV:** Jack S.
**HBP:** Ben R. 2
**WP:** Ben R., Jack S.
**Pitches-Strikes:** Ben R. 66-47, Jack S. 21-11
**Groundouts-Flyouts:** Ben R. 8-2, Jack S. 0-2
**First pitch strikes-Batters faced:** Ben R. 19-29, Jack S. 3-6

Pitching
**L:** Player 15-12
**WP:** Player 15-12, Player 15-15 2
**Pitches-Strikes:** Player 15-12 90-71, Player 15-15 21-10
**Groundouts-Flyouts:** Player 15-12 3-4, Player 15-15 0-0
**First pitch strikes-Batters faced:** Player 15-12 24-30, Player 15-15 1-5

41

# Hard 90 Clutch 12U Grabs Lead In Sixth Inning To Defeat 015 Central Florida Pride 12U

Hard 90 Clutch 12U stole the lead late in the game in an 11-9 victory over 015 Central Florida Pride 12U on Sunday. Hard 90 Clutch 12U was down 4-3 in the top of the sixth inning when Jack S homered on a 1-1 count, scoring three runs.

A seven-run lead in the sixth inning was just enough for Hard 90 Clutch 12U to hold off 015 Central Florida Pride 12U for the victory. 015 Central Florida Pride 12U scored five runs in the failed comeback on a single by Player 15-12 and a grand slam by Player 15-4.

In the first inning, 015 Central Florida Pride 12U got their offense started when an error scored two runs for 015 Central Florida Pride 12U.

Ben R was the winning pitcher for Hard 90 Clutch 12U. He went five innings, allowing eight runs on ten hits, striking out two and walking zero. Jack threw one inning in relief out of the bullpen. Jack recorded the last three outs to earn the save for Hard 90 Clutch 12U.

Player 15-12 took the loss for 015 Central Florida Pride 12U. He went five and two-thirds innings, allowing eight runs on 11 hits, striking out nine and walking one.

Hard 90 Clutch 12U hit four home runs on the day. Ben had a dinger in the sixth inning. Brady R put one out in the sixth inning. Jack went for the long ball in the sixth inning. Jordan W had a homer in the sixth inning.

Hard 90 Clutch 12U tallied 13 hits. Brady and Jack all had multiple hits for Hard 90 Clutch 12U. Brady led Hard 90 Clutch 12U with four hits in four at bats.

015 Central Florida Pride 12U tallied 11 hits on the day. Player 15-10, Player 15-9, and Player 15-12 all managed multiple hits for 015 Central Florida Pride 12U. Player 15-10 went 3-for-3 at the plate to lead 015 Central Florida Pride 12U in hits.

# 9

## COOPERSTOWN DAY 4

As the team awoke at 7:00 a.m., the boys reflected on what they needed to accomplish for the day. They made their beds, headed off to the showers, and noticed some gloomy skies.

But this did not dampen their spirits as they headed back to the barracks for their morning meeting, where they reviewed the plan for the day. At the meeting, the coaches discussed the possibility of weather delays and the need to come out with fire every time they had the opportunity.

The boys did not go to breakfast, opting instead for energy bars and more time in the batting cages.

At 11:00 a.m., the players were ready to take on the Maroons National Team from Michigan, who had gone 1-1 on the first day. The Clutch, wearing their blue uniforms, were the visiting team in this game, and they came out swinging. Jack led the game off with a hard single to left field and then Jordan hit an opposite-field tank to take a 2-0 lead. A walk, an error and a couple of singles later, and the Clutch led 4-0 after a half-inning.

Eric threw a scoreless bottom half of the first, and then the Clutch went right back to work, with Carter hitting a grand slam and Taylor adding a solo shot. At the end of two innings, the boys were up, 10-0. Once again, the Clutch had a grand opportunity to learn about respecting the game and your opponent as the team shut down their offense.

Jordan added a second home run in the top of the third inning. In a rain-soaked morning, the Clutch worked through four innings until the game was suspended with the Clutch up, 13-3.

The boys headed back to the Village for lunch at the cafeteria and proceeded to play cards—blackjack turned out to be the game of the day—as each boy learned the rules and had some friendly, fun competition. Coach Garrett also taught the boys why the house always wins in blackjack!

Hours passed as parents checked the boys out of the Village for a quick dinner before the suspended game resumed.

Before heading back to the field for an 8:30 p.m. start, the team met to once again review the importance of coming out with fire. The boys then headed down to the cages for some batting practice to get the bats going again.

In the misty evening air, Brady came on in relief and meant business, striking out three batters to end the fourth. The fifth inning was uneventful, and the Clutch led 13-4 heading into the sixth.

In that inning, Eric, Jack, and Carter added home runs to make the Hard 90 lead 19-5. With the game in hand and the opposing pitcher defeated, the Clutch learned another way to respect the opponent by playing the game within the game and practicing a two-strike pepper approach to prevent further damage.

In the home half of the sixth, a few walks allowed the Maroons to mount a small comeback, but the Clutch still won handily, 19-10.

Happy to be through the ups and downs of a rain-delayed game, the Clutch headed back to the barracks for their evening meeting, where players reflected on what they were thankful for. Things discussed included going 3-0, making it through the rain delay with energy, playing cards with teammates, and the seven home runs they'd hit that day: Carter and Jordan both smacked two, while Taylor, Eric, and Jack contributed one each.

In concluding the meeting, the Clutch discussed the importance of focusing on one game at a time, because they would be playing three games the following day. The first game, with an undefeated and very good CBA team from North Carolina, was important. The boys jotted down their goals and then headed off to sleep to the sounds of some mellow music.

| | 1 | 2 | 3 | 4 | 5 | 6 | R | H | E |
|------|---|---|---|---|---|---|----|----|---|
| CLTC | 4 | 6 | 1 | 2 | 0 | 6 | 19 | 17 | 2 |
| 051M | 0 | 1 | 2 | 1 | 0 | 6 | 10 | 7 | 4 |

Final   League Game   Cooperstown Dreams Park, Cooperstown, NY, USA

## 19 Hard 90 Clutch 12U

Monday, July 22
8:00AM

## 051 Maroons National 12U 10

### Clutch more stats

| Lineup | AB | R | H | RBI | BB | SO |
|--------|----|----|----|----|----|----|
| Jack S. | 3 | 3 | 2 | 2 | 1 | 1 |
| Jordan W. | 5 | 3 | 2 | 3 | 0 | 2 |
| Ben R. | 4 | 3 | 4 | 1 | 0 | 0 |
| Carter G. | 5 | 2 | 2 | 6 | 0 | 2 |
| Brady R. | 5 | 1 | 2 | 0 | 0 | 1 |
| Taylor S. | 5 | 3 | 2 | 2 | 0 | 1 |
| Ian P. | 2 | 0 | 1 | 0 | 0 | 1 |
| Scott B. | 1 | 1 | 0 | 0 | 0 | 0 |
| Eric E. | 4 | 1 | 1 | 2 | 0 | 1 |
| Ty M. | 2 | 1 | 0 | 0 | 0 | 2 |
| Ryan T. | 1 | 1 | 1 | 0 | 1 | 0 |
| **Totals** | **37** | **19** | **17** | **16** | **2** | **11** |

Batting
2B: Brady R.
HR: Eric E., Carter G. 2, Jack S., Taylor S., Jordan W. 2
Grand slam: Carter G.
TB: Eric E. 4, Carter G. 8, Ian P., Ben R. 4, Brady R. 3, Ryan T., Jack S. 5, Taylor S. 5, Jordan W. 8
RBI: Eric E. 2, Carter G. 6, Ben R., Jack S. 2, Taylor S. 2, Jordan W. 3
ROE: Taylor S., Jordan W.
FC: Carter G.
HBP: Scott B., Ben R., Jack S.
SB: Scott B., Ian P., Ryan T.

Totals.

Team QAB: 29 (59.62%)
Eric E. 2, Carter G. 3, Ty M., Ben R. 4, Brady R. 2, Ryan T. 2, Jack S. 4, Taylor S. 4, Jordan W. 3

Team LOB: 5

Fielding
E: Ian P., Ben R.

### 051 Maroons National 12U more stats

| Lineup | AB | R | H | RBI | BB | SO |
|--------|----|----|----|----|----|----|
| Player 51-8 | 3 | 1 | 0 | 0 | 1 | 3 |
| Player 51-7 | 3 | 1 | 1 | 2 | 0 | 1 |
| Player 51-6 | 1 | 1 | 1 | 0 | 1 | 0 |
| Player 51-12 | 1 | 1 | 0 | 0 | 2 | 0 |
| Player 51-5 | 3 | 1 | 1 | 2 | 0 | 1 |
| Player 51-3 | 2 | 2 | 1 | 1 | 1 | 0 |
| Player 51-9 | 2 | 1 | 1 | 0 | 1 | 1 |
| Player 51-2 | 2 | 1 | 0 | 1 | 1 | 1 |
| Player 51-10 | 3 | 1 | 1 | 1 | 0 | 1 |
| Player 51-11 | 3 | 0 | 0 | 0 | 0 | 1 |
| Player 51-4 | 3 | 0 | 1 | 0 | 0 | 0 |
| **Totals** | **26** | **10** | **7** | **7** | **7** | **9** |

Batting
HR: Player 51-3, Player 51-5, Player 51-7
TB: Player 51-3 4, Player 51-4, Player 51-5 4, Player 51-6, Player 51-7 4, Player 51-9, Player 51-10
RBI: Player 51-2, Player 51-3, Player 51-5 2, Player 51-7 2, Player 51-10
ROE: Player 51-4
HBP: Player 51-6
SB: Player 51-3

Totals

Team QAB: 16 (47.06%)
Player 51-2 2, Player 51-3 2, Player 51-5 2, Player 51-6 2, Player 51-7, Player 51-8, Player 51-9 2, Player 51-10, Player 51-11, Player 51-12 2

Team LOB: 6

Fielding
E: Player 51-2, Player 51-3, Player 51-7, Player 51-9
DP: Player 51-8

### Clutch more stats

| Pitching | IP | #P | S% | H | R | ER | SO | BB | HR |
|----------|----|----|----|----|----|----|----|----|----|
| Eric E. | 3.0 | 62 | .661 | 5 | 4 | 4 | 3 | 2 | 3 |
| Brady R. | 2.0 | 21 | .905 | 1 | 0 | 0 | 5 | 0 | 0 |
| Ian P. | 0.1 | 30 | .267 | 0 | 5 | 3 | 0 | 5 | 0 |
| Ty M. | 0.2 | 10 | .800 | 1 | 1 | 0 | 1 | 0 | 0 |
| **Totals** | **6.0** | **123** | **.618** | **7** | **10** | **7** | **9** | **7** | **3** |

Pitching
W: Eric E.
HBP: Eric E.
Pitches-Strikes: Eric E. 62-41, Ty M. 10-8, Ian P. 30-8, Brady R. 21-19
Groundouts-Flyouts: Eric E. 1-6, Ty M. 0-1, Ian P. 1-0, Brady R. 0-1
First pitch strikes-Batters faced: Eric E. 12-17, Ty M. 3-4, Ian P. 1-6, Brady R. 5-7

### 051 Maroons National 12U more stats

| Pitching | IP | #P | S% | H | R | ER | SO | BB | HR |
|----------|----|----|----|----|----|----|----|----|----|
| Player 51-8 | 1.0 | 43 | .512 | 5 | 9 | 5 | 3 | 1 | 2 |
| Player 51-3 | 3.0 | 66 | .606 | 4 | 4 | 3 | 6 | 1 | 2 |
| Player 51-4 | 2.0 | 37 | .649 | 8 | 6 | 6 | 2 | 0 | 3 |
| **Totals** | **6.0** | **146** | **.589** | **17** | **19** | **13** | **11** | **2** | **7** |

Pitching
L: Player 51-3
HBP: Player 51-3 2, Player 51-8
WP: Player 51-3 2, Player 51-8 2
Pitches-Strikes: Player 51-3 60-40, Player 51-4 37-24, Player 51-8 43-22
Groundouts-Flyouts: Player 51-3 3-0, Player 51-4 0-2, Player 51-8 1-0
First pitch strikes-Batters faced: Player 51-3 6-16, Player 51-4 7-13, Player 51-8 4-13

# R. Collects Four Hits As Hard 90 Clutch 12U Defeats 051 Maroons National 12U

Ben R got busy on the basepaths on Monday, knocking four hits in Hard 90 Clutch 12U's 19-10 victory over 051 Maroons National 12U. Ben singled in the first, singled in the third, singled in the fifth, and singled in the sixth.

051 Maroons National 12U scored six runs in the sixth inning, but Hard 90 Clutch 12U still managed to pull out the victory. The big inning for 051 Maroons National 12U came thanks to a walk by Player 51-2, a single by Player 51-10, a groundout by Player 51-5, and an error on a ball put in play by Player 51-4.

Hard 90 Clutch 12U got things moving in the first inning, when Jordan W homered on a 1-0 count, scoring two runs.

Eric E was credited with the victory for Hard 90 Clutch 12U. He surrendered four runs on five hits over three innings, striking out three. Brady R, Ty M, and Ian P all put in work in relief out of the bullpen, steering their team towards the victory.

Player 51-3 took the loss for 051 Maroons National 12U. He surrendered four runs on four hits over three innings, striking out six and walking one.

Player 51-8 started the game for 051 Maroons National 12U. He surrendered nine runs on five hits over one inning, striking out three and walking one

Hard 90 Clutch 12U tallied seven home runs on the day. Carter G had a long ball in the second and sixth innings. Eric went for the long ball in the sixth inning. Jack S put one out in the sixth inning. Jordan had a dinger in the first and third innings. Taylor S had a homer in the second inning.

Hard 90 Clutch 12U racked up 17 hits. Ben, Brady, Carter, Jordan, Jack, and Taylor all collected multiple hits for Hard 90 Clutch 12U. Ben went 4-for-4 at the plate to lead Hard 90 Clutch 12U in hits.

# 10

## COOPERSTOWN DAY 5

The Hard 90 Clutch had an early start on Day 5, needing to play three games in one day. Wake up came at 6:30AM. While the skies were overcast, the sun was peeking through offering the promise of a great day of baseball.

Once again, the boys saw the importance of the consistent 7:00AM wake up to be able to manage an early start. The boys quickly reflected on what they needed to accomplish for the day, showered, downed an energy bar, and then headed off to the batting cages.

As the team walked to the field for our meeting with CBA, it was unclear what effect the late-night game would have on the boys. The Clutch was the home team and CBA came to play. With a couple of home runs to start the game and some fielding errors, the boys found themselves down 5-0 with no outs in the first inning.

At this point, the coaches brought in Jordan to pitch and he was able to get the Clutch out of the inning with a pickoff, a strikeout, and a ground ball.

One of the themes for the Clutch the entire year was accountability to each other. Some of the players had a tough time with the quick turnaround and were removed from the game. This is a big life lesson that we teach at Hard 90: Do your very best by being ready to play, regardless of the circumstances.

CBA clearly had their #1 pitcher on the mound, sporting a fastball in the low 70s with a strong off-speed pitch. Two Ks and a popout and the Clutch was back on defense. Lucky for us, Jordan held serve with a K and two groundouts.

Heading into the bottom of the second, the Clutch was still down 5-0—but that changed in the first at-bat. Carter took a monstrous hack on the first pitch and fouled it straight back. One of the things that we worked on as a team was an aggressive approach at the plate—"big-daddy hacks" as the team called them—so the entire Clutch team encouraged Carter to stay aggressive. There it was on the next pitch: Carter hit a tank way over the left field fence, and the Clutch was on the board.

One batter later, Taylor also connected on a big-daddy hack. CBA still led 5-2, but you could feel the momentum of the game subtly shifting.

Two more Ks and a pickoff and Jordan had the Clutch back in the dugout to hit again. Back at the top of the order, singles by Jordan and Ben put Carter at the plate with two outs and a chance to tie the ball game. He wasted no time, smashing a no-doubter over the centerfield fence to tie the game 5-5. It was a new ball game and the momentum had clearly shifted.

With the score still 5-5 in the bottom of the fifth, Captain Jack stepped up to the plate with one thing on his mind—you guessed it—big-daddy hacks. Jack hit a bomb that cleared the left field fence by 50 feet, giving the Clutch their first lead of the game.

With the Clutch leading 6-5 and Jordan at 65 pitches, the Clutch coaches had a brief conversation as to whether he should pitch the sixth. Coach Devon, Jordan's older brother, quickly stated that it was Jordan's game to close.

In the top of the sixth, Jordan came out with fire and struck out the first batter. The next batter popped out on the first pitch. The Clutch was now one out away from a remarkable comeback. Jordan fired three pitches across the plate for a strikeout, and the Clutch sealed the win. It was a huge victory with some big-time performances by Carter, Taylor, and Jack with clutch home runs and six no-hit innings by Jordan, who recorded 10 Ks.

With this emotional victory under their belts, the Clutch headed back to the barracks to change and have a brief team celebration. The celebration included a bit of dancing to "California Love" to celebrate a 4-0 start.

The team checked out of the Village and headed to Barnyard Swing for some team bonding over mini golf and then back to Maskot's for lunch. Given the close victory and exciting comeback, energy was high and the boys were reveling in their time at Cooperstown.

At 1:30 p.m, the Clutch reported back to the field to take on the Midland Park Panthers from New Jersey. There was a ton of buzz around the park about this great hitting team from California that was undefeated heading into game 5.

The Clutch started on offense and Captain Jack once again did his job, swinging hard at the second pitch and sending it into orbit. A message that we worked on for months was that if you were going to beat the Clutch in Cooperstown, you were going to have to out-hit us, because we were going to swing the bat.

At the end of two innings, the score was tied 1-1. Then Ryan blasted his first home run of the tournament to start the third, Jack added another, Jordan singled, and Ben notched his second dinger of the tournament. A few batters later, Scotty got in the action with his first long ball of the tournament, and suddenly it was 9-1.

Ryan shut the door in the bottom of the third, and it was 10-1 heading into the 4th. In the top of the 4th, Ian had a nice double to make it 11-1.

The rest of the fourth was relatively uneventful, and it was 12-3 heading into the fifth, when Ty blasted a bomb on the first inning's first pitch. Two batters later, Carter hit a two-run home run. A few singles later and Ty found himself at the plate with the bases loaded, and he promptly hit a moonshot for a grand slam and his second home run of the inning. With the game out of hand, the Clutch again exercised restraint and started working on a two-strike approach with a game of pepper to end the inning.

Ryan again shut the Panthers down in the fifth and the Clutch was 5-0 with a 20-3 victory.

The team then headed back to the barracks to get ready for their final pool-play game, which was to begin at 6:30 p.m. against the Horsham Hounds from Pennsylvania.

Brady started the scoring with a home run in the bottom of the second. A few batters later, Ty laced a two-run shot. Not to be outdone, Jack, Jordan, and Ryan also all homered to make it 8-0 after two complete innings.

Ty pitched a scoreless third and Taylor and Eric added home runs to make it 10-0. In the fifth, the Clutch called upon their catcher Scotty to pitch his first inning of the year. Scotty threw a great frame, only surrendering one run. With Scotty taking the mound, every Hard 90 Clutch player had pitched in the Cooperstown Dreams Park tournament.

In the bottom of the fifth, the Clutch had the opportunity to participate in the spirit of Cooperstown Dreams Park. The Hounds had a pitcher that had not yet pitched in Cooperstown, but the coach was concerned with safety after seeing how hard our team hit the ball. The Clutch responded by peppering away the fifth, allowing this pitcher an opportunity of a lifetime to experience the mound at Cooperstown. Later that evening, the pitcher's dad found one of the Clutch coaches and thanked him for allowing his son to experience this opportunity.

With the 10-5 win, the Clutch had gone 6-0 in pool play, earning the 10th seed out of 104 teams and all the while respecting the game and their opponents.

After the last game of the day, the Clutch had a team dinner at Redneck BBQ. It was so fun to sit back and watch the boys bond over another meal. This group had grinded it out over the last three years with tough workouts and ups and downs on the field, and here they were living the dream in Cooperstown.

At 10 p.m. the team reported for their evening meeting. After reflecting on the day, the number one thing the boys were thankful for was accomplishing their stated goal of going 6-0 in pool play. They were also grateful for the time to hang out—and of course to hit more home runs.

The Clutch hit a total of 19 home runs that day: Jack hit four, Carter and Ty each had three, Ryan and Taylor slammed two apiece, and Ben, Brady, Eric, Jordan, and Scott added one each.

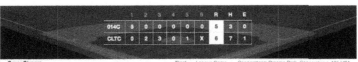

| | 1 | 2 | 3 | 4 | 5 | 6 | R | H | E |
|---|---|---|---|---|---|---|---|---|---|
| 014C | 5 | 0 | 0 | 0 | 0 | 0 | 5 | 3 | 0 |
| CLTC | 0 | 2 | 3 | 0 | 1 | X | 6 | 7 | 1 |

**GameStream**  Final  League Game  Cooperstown Dreams Park, Cooperstown, NY, USA

**5** 014 CBA Copperheads Black 12U

Tuesday, July 23
5:30AM

Hard 90 Clutch 12U **6**

Game Highlights | **Box Score** | Away Stats | Home Stats | Plays | Scorebook | Recap Story

### 014 CBA Copperheads Black 12U more stats

| Lineup | AB | R | H | RBI | BB | SO |
|---|---|---|---|---|---|---|
| Player 14-7 | 1 | 1 | 1 | 1 | 0 | 0 |
| Player 14-6 | 1 | 1 | 0 | 0 | 1 | 1 |
| Player 14-5 | 2 | 1 | 1 | 2 | 0 | 1 |
| #15 | 2 | 1 | 1 | 0 | 0 | 0 |
| Player 14-3 | 2 | 1 | 0 | 0 | 0 | 2 |
| Player 14-4 | 1 | 0 | 0 | 0 | 1 | 0 |
| Player 14-13 | 2 | 0 | 0 | 0 | 0 | 1 |
| Player 14-10 | 2 | 0 | 0 | 0 | 0 | 1 |
| Player 14-9 | 2 | 0 | 0 | 0 | 0 | 2 |
| Player 14-8 | 2 | 0 | 0 | 0 | 0 | 0 |
| Player 14-12 | 2 | 0 | 0 | 0 | 0 | 1 |
| Player 14-11 | 1 | 0 | 0 | 0 | 0 | 1 |
| **Totals** | **20** | **5** | **3** | **3** | **2** | **10** |

Batting
HR: Player 14-7, Player 14-5
TB: Player 14-7 4, Player 14-5 4, #15
RBI: Player 14-7, Player 14-5 2
HBP: Player 14-7
SB: Player 14-7, #15
CS: Player 14-4
PIK: Player 14-7

Totals
Team QAB: 15 (65.22%)
Player 14-10, Player 14-11, Player 14-12, Player 14-13, Player 14-3, Player 14-6 2, Player 14-7, Player 14-9, Player 14-4 2, Player 14-5 2, #15 2

Team LOB: 0

### Clutch more stats

| Lineup | AB | R | H | RBI | BB | SO |
|---|---|---|---|---|---|---|
| Jack S. | 3 | 1 | 1 | 1 | 0 | 1 |
| Jordan W. | 3 | 1 | 1 | 0 | 0 | 1 |
| Ben R. | 3 | 1 | 1 | 0 | 0 | 0 |
| Carter G. | 3 | 2 | 2 | 4 | 0 | 1 |
| Brady R. | 2 | 0 | 1 | 0 | 0 | 0 |
| Taylor S. | 2 | 1 | 1 | 1 | 0 | 1 |
| Eric E. | 1 | 0 | 0 | 0 | 0 | 1 |
| Ian P. | 1 | 0 | 0 | 0 | 0 | 0 |
| Ryan T. | 2 | 0 | 0 | 0 | 0 | 0 |
| Ty M. | 2 | 0 | 0 | 0 | 0 | 0 |
| Scott B. | . | . | . | . | . | . |
| **Totals** | **22** | **6** | **7** | **6** | **0** | **6** |

Batting
HR: Carter G. 2, Jack S., Taylor S.
TB: Carter G. 8, Ben R., Brady R., Jack S. 4, Taylor S. 4, Jordan W.
RBI: Carter G. 4, Jack S., Taylor S.

Totals
Team QAB: 10 (45.46%)
Carter G. 2, Ty M., Ben R., Brady R., Jack S. 2, Taylor S. 2, Jordan W.

Team LOB: 1

Fielding
E: Scott B.

### 014 CBA Copperheads Black 12U more stats

| Pitching | IP | #P | S% | H | R | ER | SO | BB | HR |
|---|---|---|---|---|---|---|---|---|---|
| Player 14-9 | 5.0 | 63 | .778 | 7 | 6 | 6 | 5 | 0 | 4 |
| **Totals** | **5.0** | **63** | **.778** | **7** | **6** | **6** | **5** | **0** | **4** |

Pitching
L: Player 14-9
Pitches-Strikes: Player 14-9 63-49
Groundouts-Flyouts: Player 14-9 3-7
First pitch strikes-Batters faced: Player 14-9 18-22

### Clutch more stats

| Pitching | IP | #P | S% | H | R | ER | SO | BB | HR |
|---|---|---|---|---|---|---|---|---|---|
| Ryan T. | 0.0 | 17 | .588 | 3 | 4 | 4 | 0 | 1 | 2 |
| Jordan W. | 6.0 | 77 | .636 | 0 | 1 | 0 | 10 | 1 | 0 |
| **Totals** | **6.0** | **94** | **.628** | **3** | **5** | **4** | **10** | **2** | **2** |

Pitching
W: Jordan W.
HBP: Jordan W.
WP: Jordan W.
Pitches-Strikes: Ryan T. 17-10, Jordan W. 77-49
Groundouts-Flyouts: Ryan T. 0-0, Jordan W. 4-3
First pitch strikes-Batters faced: Ryan T. 3-4, Jordan W. 10-19

# Hard 90 Clutch 12U Claims Lead In Fifth Inning To Defeat 014 CBA Copperheads Black 12U

Hard 90 Clutch 12U stole the lead late in the game in a 6-5 victory over 014 CBA Copperheads Black 12U on Tuesday. The game was tied at five with Hard 90 Clutch 12U batting in the bottom of the fifth when Jack S hit a solo homer.

Hard 90 Clutch 12U earned the victory despite allowing 014 CBA Copperheads Black 12U to score five runs in the first inning. 014 CBA Copperheads Black 12U's big inning was driven by home runs by Player 14-7 and Player14-5.

014 CBA Copperheads Black 12U got things moving in the first inning. Player 14-7 hit a solo homer.

Hard 90 Clutch 12U evened things up at five in the bottom of the third inning. Hard 90 Clutch 12U scored three runs when Carter G homered.

Hard 90 Clutch 12U scored three runs in the third inning. Hard 90 Clutch 12U scored its runs on a home run by Carter.

Jordan W earned the win for Hard 90 Clutch 12U. He surrendered one run on zero hits over six innings, striking out ten and walking one.

Player 14-9 took the loss for 014 CBA Copperheads Black 12U. He lasted five innings, allowing seven hits and six runs while striking out five and walking zero.

Ryan T started the game for Hard 90 Clutch 12U. He surrendered four runs on three hits, walking one

Hard 90 Clutch 12U hit four home runs on the day. Carter went yard in the second and third innings. Jack went for the long ball in the fifth inning. Taylor S went deep in the second inning.

Carter led Hard 90 Clutch 12U with two hits in three at bats.

014 CBA Copperheads Black 12U was sure-handed in the field and didn't commit a single error. #15 had the most chances in the field with five.

|       | 1 | 2 | 3 | 4 | 5 | 6 | R | H | E |
|-------|---|---|---|---|---|---|---|---|---|
| CLTC  | 1 | 0 | 9 | 2 | 8 | X | 20 | 20 | 1 |
| MDLN  | 1 | 0 | 0 | 2 | 0 | X | 3 | 5 | 3 |

GameStream  Final  League Game  Cooperstown Dreams Park, Cooperstown, NY, USA

## 20 Hard 90 Clutch 12U

Tuesday, July 23
11:30AM

## Midland Park Panthers 12U  3

| Lineup | AB | R | H | RBI | BB | SO |
|--------|----|---|---|-----|----|----|
| Jack S. | 2 | 2 | 2 | 2 | 0 | 0 |
| Eric E. | 3 | 2 | 2 | 1 | 0 | 0 |
| Jordan W. | 2 | 3 | 1 | 0 | 0 | 0 |
| Ty M. | 3 | 2 | 3 | 6 | 0 | 0 |
| Ben R. | 5 | 2 | 2 | 0 | 0 | 0 |
| Carter G. | 3 | 3 | 1 | 2 | 1 | 0 |
| Brady R. | 4 | 2 | 2 | 0 | 0 | 0 |
| Taylor S. | 4 | 1 | 2 | 2 | 0 | 1 |
| Scott B. | 4 | 1 | 1 | 2 | 0 | 0 |
| Ian R. | 4 | 1 | 2 | 1 | 0 | 0 |
| Ryan T. | 4 | 1 | 2 | 2 | 0 | 0 |
| Totals | 38 | 20 | 20 | 20 | 1 | 1 |

Batting
2B: Ian R.
HR: Scott B., Carter G., Ty M. 2, Ben R., Ryan T., Jack S. 2
Grand slam: Ty M.
TB: Scott B. 4, Eric E. 2, Carter G. 4, Ty M. 9, Ian R. 3, Ben R. 5, Brady R. 2, Ryan T. 6, Jack S. 8, Taylor S. 2, Jordan W.
RBI: Scott B. 2, Eric E., Carter G. 2, Ty M. 6, Ian R., Ben R. 2, Ryan T. 2, Jack S. 2, Taylor S. 2
ROE: Scott B. 2, Carter G.
FC: Eric E.

Totals
Team QAB: 20 (51.28%)
Scott B., Eric E., Carter G. 3, Ty M. 3, Ian R. 2, Ben R., Brady R. 2, Ryan T., Jack S. 2, Taylor S. 3, Jordan W.

Team LOB: 3

Fielding
E: Brady R.

| Lineup | AB | R | H | RBI | BB | SO |
|--------|----|---|---|-----|----|----|
| #13 | 2 | 0 | 0 | 0 | 0 | 0 |
| #h | 2 | 1 | 1 | 0 | 0 | 0 |
| #9 | 2 | 2 | 2 | 3 | 0 | 0 |
| #14 | 2 | 0 | 1 | 0 | 0 | 0 |
| #6 | 2 | 0 | 0 | 0 | 0 | 2 |
| #3 | 2 | 0 | 0 | 0 | 0 | 0 |
| #8 | 2 | 0 | 0 | 0 | 0 | 1 |
| #15 | 2 | 0 | 1 | 0 | 0 | 0 |
| #1 | 2 | 0 | 0 | 0 | 0 | 1 |
| #7 | 1 | 0 | 0 | 0 | 0 | 0 |
| #11 | 1 | 0 | 0 | 0 | 0 | 0 |
| #4 | 1 | 0 | 0 | 0 | 0 | 0 |
| #2 | 0 | 0 | 0 | 0 | 0 | 0 |
| Conor S. | - | - | - | - | - | - |
| Aiden D. | - | - | - | - | - | - |
| Jack D. | - | - | - | - | - | - |
| Totals | 21 | 3 | 5 | 3 | 0 | 4 |

Batting
HR: #9 2
TB: #14, #5, #9 8, #15
RBI: #9 3
ROE: #7
SB: #14, #2

Totals
Team QAB: 4 (19.05%)
#9 2, #8, #11

Team LOB: 3

### Clutch more stats

| Pitching | IP | #P | S% | H | R | ER | SO | BB | HR |
|----------|----|----|----|----|---|----|----|----|----|
| Ryan T. | 5.0 | 65 | .754 | 5 | 3 | 3 | 4 | 0 | 2 |
| Totals | 5.0 | 65 | .754 | 5 | 3 | 3 | 4 | 0 | 2 |

Pitching
W: Ryan T.
Pitches-Strikes: Ryan T. 65-49
Groundouts-Flyouts: Ryan T. 8-3
First pitch strikes-Batters faced: Ryan T. 15-21

### Midland Park Panthers 12U more stats

| Pitching | IP | #P | S% | H | R | ER | SO | BB | HR |
|----------|----|----|----|----|---|----|----|----|----|
| #1 | 2.0 | 35 | .714 | 8 | 8 | 8 | 0 | 1 | 4 |
| #5 | 3.0 | 48 | .750 | 12 | 12 | 4 | 1 | 0 | 4 |
| Totals | 5.0 | 83 | .735 | 20 | 20 | 12 | 1 | 1 | 8 |

Pitching
L: #1
WP: #1 3
Pitches-Strikes: #1 35-25, #5 48-36
Groundouts-Flyouts: #1 3-3, #5 4-3
First pitch strikes-Batters faced: #1 11-15, #5 18-24

# 90 Clutch 12U's Victory Over Midland Park Panthers 12U

Ty M was bad news for opposing pitchers on Tuesday, driving in six on three hits to lead Hard 90 Clutch 12U past Midland Park Panthers 12U 20-3 on Tuesday. Ty drove in runs on a single in the third, a home run in the fifth, and a grand slam in the fifth.

Hard 90 Clutch 12U got things moving in the first inning, when Jack S hit a solo homer.

Midland Park Panthers 12U knotted the game up at one in the bottom of the first inning, when #9 hit a solo homer.

After Hard 90 Clutch 12U scored two runs in the top of the fourth, Midland Park Panthers 12U answered with two of their own. Hard 90 Clutch 12U scored when Ian P doubled on the first pitch of the at bat, scoring one run and Ryan T singled on a 1-0 count, scoring one run. Midland Park Panthers 12U then answered when #9 homered on a 0-1 count, scoring two runs.

Hard 90 Clutch 12U pulled away for good with nine runs in the third inning. In the third Ryan hit a solo homer, Jack hit a solo homer, Ben R homered on a 2-2 count, scoring two runs, Taylor S singled on a 1-2 count, scoring two runs, Scott B homered on the first pitch of the at bat, scoring two runs, and Ty singled on a 2-2 count, scoring one run.

Ryan was the winning pitcher for Hard 90 Clutch 12U. He allowed five hits and three runs over five innings, striking out four and walking zero.

#1 took the loss for Midland Park Panthers 12U. He went two innings, allowing eight runs on eight hits and walking one.

Hard 90 Clutch 12U launched eight home runs on the day. Ben went for the long ball in the third inning. Carter G had a four bagger in the fifth inning. Jack went for the long ball in the first and third innings. Ryan went yard in the third inning. Scott had a four bagger in the third inning. Ty went deep in the fifth and fifth innings.

Hard 90 Clutch 12U collected 20 hits on the day. Ty, Ian, Ryan , Brady R, Ben, Eric E, Jack, and Taylor all collected multiple hits for Hard 90 Clutch 12U. Ty went 3-for-3 at the plate to lead Hard 90 Clutch 12U in hits.

#9 led Midland Park Panthers 12U with two hits in two at bats.

| | 1 | 2 | 3 | 4 | 5 | 6 | R | H | E |
|---|---|---|---|---|---|---|---|---|---|
| 037H | 0 | 0 | 0 | 1 | 1 | 3 | 5 | 8 | 1 |
| CLTC | 0 | 8 | 2 | 0 | 0 | X | 10 | 11 | 1 |

**GameStream**  Final  League Game  Cooperstown Dreams Park, Cooperstown, NY, USA

## 5  037 Horsham Hounds Black 12U

Tuesday, July 23
3:30PM

## Hard 90 Clutch 12U  10

### 037 Horsham Hounds Black 12U more stats

| Lineup | AB | R | H | RBI | BB | SO |
|---|---|---|---|---|---|---|
| #142 | 1 | 0 | 0 | 0 | 0 | 0 |
| #2 | 0 | 0 | 0 | 0 | 1 | 0 |
| #3 | 1 | 0 | 1 | 1 | 0 | 0 |
| #4 | 1 | 0 | 0 | 0 | 0 | 0 |
| #5 | 1 | 0 | 0 | 0 | 0 | 0 |
| #6 | 0 | 1 | 0 | 0 | 0 | 0 |
| #7 | 1 | 0 | 0 | 0 | 0 | 0 |
| #8 | 1 | 0 | 0 | 1 | 0 | 0 |
| #9 | 1 | 0 | 0 | 0 | 0 | 0 |
| #10 | 1 | 1 | 1 | 0 | 0 | 0 |
| #11 | 1 | 1 | 1 | 0 | 0 | 0 |
| #15 | 0 | 1 | 0 | 0 | 1 | 0 |
| #14 | 2 | 0 | 1 | 2 | 0 | 0 |
| #12 | 2 | 0 | 1 | 0 | 0 | 1 |
| Player 37-12 | 2 | 0 | 1 | 0 | 0 | 0 |
| Player 37-4 | 2 | 0 | 0 | 0 | 0 | 1 |
| Player 37-1 | 2 | 0 | 0 | 0 | 0 | 1 |
| Player 37-13 | 1 | 0 | 0 | 0 | 0 | 1 |
| Player 37-9 | 1 | 0 | 0 | 0 | 0 | 0 |
| Player 37-10 | 1 | 0 | 0 | 0 | 0 | 0 |
| Player 37-3 | 1 | 0 | 0 | 0 | 0 | 0 |
| Player 37-15 | 1 | 1 | 1 | 0 | 0 | 0 |

### Clutch more stats

| Lineup | AB | R | H | RBI | BB | SO |
|---|---|---|---|---|---|---|
| Ian P. | 3 | 1 | 1 | 0 | 0 | 0 |
| Jack S. | 3 | 1 | 2 | 2 | 0 | 0 |
| Jordan W. | 3 | 1 | 1 | 1 | 0 | 1 |
| Ben R. | 1 | 0 | 0 | 0 | 0 | 0 |
| Scott B. | 2 | 1 | 1 | 0 | 0 | 0 |
| Carter G. | 1 | 0 | 0 | 0 | 0 | 0 |
| Ryan T. | 1 | 1 | 1 | 2 | 1 | 0 |
| Brady R. | 3 | 1 | 1 | 1 | 0 | 1 |
| Taylor S. | 2 | 2 | 1 | 1 | 1 | 0 |
| Eric E. | 3 | 1 | 1 | 1 | 0 | 1 |
| Ty M. | 3 | 1 | 2 | 2 | 0 | 0 |
| Totals | 25 | 10 | 11 | 10 | 2 | 3 |

**Batting**
HR: Eric E., Ty M., Brady R., Ryan T., Jack S., Taylor S., Jordan W.
TB: Scott B., Eric E. 4, Ty M. 5, Ian P., Brady R. 4, Ryan T. 4, Jack S. 5, Taylor S. 4, Jordan W. 4.
RBI: Eric E., Ty M. 2, Brady R., Ryan T. 2, Jack S. 2, Taylor S., Jordan W.
ROE: Ian P.
GIDP: Ian P.
SB: Scott B., Taylor S.

Totals
Team QAB: 10 (58.26%)
Scott B. 2, Eric E. 3, Ty M., Ian P., Brady R. 2, Ryan T. 2, Jack S. 2, Taylor S. 2, Jordan W.

Team LOB: 2

Fielding
E: Jack S.
DP: Jack S.

### 037 Horsham Hounds Black 12U more stats

| Pitching | IP | #P | S% | H | R | ER | SO | BB | HR |
|---|---|---|---|---|---|---|---|---|---|
| #4 | 5.0 | 91 | .626 | 11 | 10 | 10 | 3 | 2 | 7 |
| Totals | 5.0 | 91 | .626 | 11 | 10 | 10 | 3 | 2 | 7 |

Pitching
Pitches-Strikes: #4 91-57
Groundouts-Flyouts: #4 6-4
First pitch strikes-Batters faced: #4 17-27

### Clutch more stats

| Pitching | IP | #P | S% | H | R | ER | SO | BB | HR |
|---|---|---|---|---|---|---|---|---|---|
| Brady R. | 2.0 | 16 | .875 | 0 | 0 | 0 | 2 | 0 | 0 |
| Ty M. | 2.0 | 30 | .600 | 3 | 1 | 1 | 0 | 1 | 0 |
| Scott B. | 1.0 | 13 | .538 | 0 | 1 | 1 | 0 | 0 | 0 |
| Jack S. | 1.0 | 37 | .649 | 5 | 3 | 3 | 2 | 1 | 0 |
| Totals | 6.0 | 96 | .666 | 8 | 5 | 5 | 4 | 2 | 0 |

Pitching
HBP: Scott B.
WP: Jack S.
Pitches-Strikes: Scott B. 13-7, Ty M. 30-18, Brady R. 16-14, Jack S. 37-24
Groundouts-Flyouts: Scott B. 2-1, Ty M. 3-3, Brady R. 2-1, Jack S. 0-0
First pitch strikes-Batters faced: Scott B. 2-4, Ty M. 9-10, Brady R. 6-6, Jack S. 5-8

# Hard 90 Clutch 12U Defeats 037 Horsham Hounds Black 12U Despite Allowing 3-Run Inning

Despite allowing three runs in the sixth inning, Hard 90 Clutch 12U defeated 037 Horsham Hounds Black 12U 10-5 on Tuesday. #14 and #12 powered the big inning with RBIs.

Brady R was on the pitcher's mound for Hard 90 Clutch 12U. He went two innings, allowing zero runs on zero hits, striking out two and walking zero.

#4 started the game for 037 Horsham Hounds Black 12U. He went five innings, allowing ten runs on 11 hits and striking out three.

Hard 90 Clutch 12U smacked seven home runs on the day. Brady put one out in the second inning. Eric E had a long ball in the third inning. Jack S went yard in the second inning. Jordan W had a dinger in the second inning. Ryan T. put one out in the second inning. Taylor S had a homer in the third inning. Ty M went for the long ball in the second inning.

Hard 90 Clutch 12U racked up 11 hits in the game. Ty and Jack each managed multiple hits for Hard 90 Clutch 12U. Jack and Ty each collected two hits to lead Hard 90 Clutch 12U.

# 11

## Cooperstown Day 6

While the boys earned the opportunity to sleep in, they found out that when you have to wake up at the same time every day, you naturally wake up that time even when you don't have to. All the boys woke up between 7:00 and 7:30 to a beautiful and sunny Cooperstown morning.

After reviewing the keys to success for the day, the kids made their beds and headed to the showers. They then gathered for a brief meeting before heading out to the cafeteria for breakfast.

At 9:15 a.m., all the boys were checked out of the village and headed to the Hall of Fame, where they gathered in front for a team picture before heading into the Hall.

The first destination was the theater where the boys watched a special production on Hall of Famers "Generations of the Game" and what the game meant to them. The movie was an incredible tribute to baseball by the sport's legends.

After the movie, the team headed off in groups, many with their fathers and mothers, to tour the Hall of Fame. The Clutch is made up of baseball families—Red Sox fans,

Giants fans, Cubs fans, and, yes, Yankees fans—so each area of the Hall meant something different to each family. The coaches thoroughly enjoyed watching 11 young men who have grown up in the game together tour baseball's hallowed ground and seeing what portion of the Hall was special to them.

After a few hours in the Hall, team members headed to lunch before a mandatory 2:30 meeting back at the barracks.

In the meeting, the boys reviewed what they needed to do to be successful in the game and to come out with some fire. At 4:30, the team headed to the batting cages to start to prepare for their first elimination game.

At 6:30, it was on. The Hard 90 Clutch was taking on the Louisiana Blues. The Blues were coming off an exciting win and this was the Clutch's first bracket game.

On the mound for the Clutch was their ace, Ben. The Clutch was the home team. There were definitely some nerves and in the top of the first, the Blues put up two runs.

The Clutch responded per usual: Jack led off with a hard swing for a base hit to left field, and then Jordan hit a moonshot over the right field fence to tie the game.

Ben settled in to throw a scoreless second, and Scotty got the party started for the Clutch, hitting the first pitch he saw over the fence. Two batters later Ty hit a bomb. Clutch 4, Blues 2, after two innings.

After yielding a run in the top of the third, the Clutch home-run party resumed. Brady and Taylor went back-to-back, making it 7-3, Clutch, after three.

After the Blues scored two in the top of the fourth to make it 7-5, Blues fans were seeing the light and getting feisty—but the Clutch answered. Sparking the action was a cheering battle in the outfield between two Blues dads and the Sisters of Clutch—a group of younger sisters that accompanied the boys on their trip to Cooperstown.

Seeing this excitement beyond the outfield fence, the Clutch decided that they better squash the momentum; Jack and Jordan led off the inning with back-to-back rockets way over the fence. After a few more singles, up stepped Ryan, who blasted a three-run bomb on a 3-0 count. Two batters later, Jack hit his second home run of the inning, making it 16-3 after four.

Ben shut the door in the top of the fifth, and Brady hit a bomb in the bottom of the inning, ending the game at 17-5. The Clutch hit 10 homers in the first bracket game.

The team was happy to have their first bracket-play game behind them. After a quick meeting and talk with parents and fans, the Clutch headed back to the barracks to enjoy the rest of the evening.

The boys had their traditional 10:00 p.m. meeting that night. Highlights of the day were visiting the Hall of Fame and seeing some of their heroes, more time together with teammates, and a big bracket play win. The boys discussed what they needed to do the next day to keep the run going.

At 10:30 p.m., it was lights out.

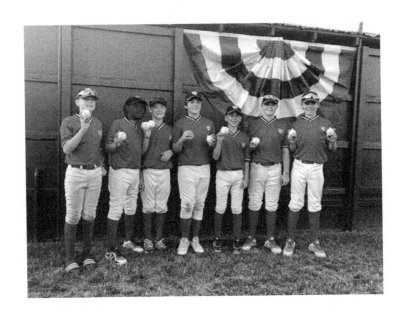

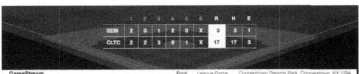

| | 1 | 2 | 3 | 4 | 5 | 6 | R | H | E |
|---|---|---|---|---|---|---|---|---|---|
| 0239 | 2 | 0 | 1 | 2 | 0 | X | 5 | 5 | 1 |
| CLTC | 2 | 2 | 3 | 9 | 1 | X | 17 | 17 | 3 |

**5**   023 985 Louisiana Blues     Wednesday, July 24   3:30PM     Hard 90 Clutch 12U   **17**

Game Highlights   **Box Score**   Away Stats   Home Stats   Plays   Scorebook   Recap Story

### 023 985 Louisiana Blues more stats

| Lineup | AB | R | H | RBI | BB | SO |
|---|---|---|---|---|---|---|
| Player 2-14 | 3 | 2 | 1 | 0 | 0 | 0 |
| Player 2-15 | 3 | 1 | 2 | 0 | 0 | 0 |
| Player 2-9 | 1 | 0 | 0 | 1 | 0 | 1 |
| Player 2-5 | 1 | 0 | 0 | 0 | 0 | 1 |
| Player 2-11 | 3 | 0 | 0 | 1 | 0 | 0 |
| Player 2-12 | 2 | 1 | 1 | 0 | 0 | 0 |
| Player 2-1 | 1 | 1 | 1 | 0 | 1 | 0 |
| Player 2-8 | 2 | 0 | 0 | 1 | 0 | 0 |
| Player 2-7 | 2 | 0 | 0 | 1 | 0 | 0 |
| Player 2-3 | 1 | 0 | 0 | 0 | 1 | 1 |
| Player 2-13 | 2 | 0 | 0 | 0 | 0 | 0 |
| **Totals** | **21** | **5** | **5** | **4** | **2** | **3** |

Batting
TB: Player 2-1, Player 2-12, Player 2-14, Player 2-15 2
RBI: Player 2-7, Player 2-8, Player 2-9, Player 2-11
SF: Player 2-9
ROE: Player 2-12, Player 2-14 2
FC: Player 2-8
SB: Player 2-14, Player 2-15

Totals
Team QAB: 9 (30.33%)
Player 2-1, Player 2-3, Player 2-9, Player 2-11, Player 2-12, Player 2-14, Player 2-15 2

Team LOB: 4

Fielding
E: Player 2-3

### Clutch more stats

| Lineup | AB | R | H | RBI | BB | SO |
|---|---|---|---|---|---|---|
| Jack S. | 4 | 3 | 3 | 3 | 0 | 0 |
| Jordan W. | 4 | 2 | 2 | 3 | 0 | 0 |
| Ben R. | 4 | 0 | 1 | 0 | 0 | 0 |
| Carter G. | 4 | 2 | 1 | 0 | 0 | 0 |
| Brady R. | 3 | 3 | 2 | 3 | 0 | 0 |
| Taylor S. | 3 | 2 | 2 | 2 | 0 | 0 |
| Scott B. | 3 | 1 | 3 | 1 | 0 | 0 |
| Eric E. | 2 | 0 | 0 | 0 | 0 | 0 |
| Ryan T. | 1 | 1 | 1 | 3 | 0 | 0 |
| Ty M. | 2 | 1 | 1 | 1 | 0 | 0 |
| Ian P. | 1 | 2 | 1 | 0 | 0 | 0 |
| **Totals** | **31** | **17** | **17** | **16** | **0** | **0** |

Batting
HR: Scott B., Ty M., Brady R. 2, Ryan T., Jack S. 2, Taylor S., Jordan W. 2
TB: Scott B. 6, Carter G., Ty M. 4, Ian P., Ben R., Brady R. 8, Ryan T. 4, Jack S. 9, Taylor S. 5, Jordan W. 8
RBI: Scott B., Ty M., Brady R. 3, Ryan T. 3, Jack S. 3, Taylor S. 2, Jordan W. 3
ROE: Carter G.
HBP: Brady R.
SB: Ian P.

Totals
Team QAB: 18 (60.00%)
Scott B. 2, Eric E., Carter G., Ty M., Ben R., Brady R. 2, Ryan T., Jack S. 3, Taylor S. 2, Jordan W. 2

Team LOB: 2

Fielding
E: Carter G., Jack S., Taylor S.

### 023 985 Louisiana Blues more stats

| Pitching | IP | #P | S% | H | R | ER | SO | BB | HR |
|---|---|---|---|---|---|---|---|---|---|
| Player 2-1 | 2.1 | 38 | .714 | 6 | 6 | 5 | 0 | 0 | 4 |
| Player 2-12 | 0.2 | 20 | .550 | 4 | 3 | 3 | 0 | 0 | 3 |
| Player 2-13 | 0.1 | 19 | .579 | 4 | 5 | 5 | 0 | 0 | 1 |
| Player 2-14 | 1.0 | 19 | .684 | 3 | 3 | 3 | 0 | 0 | 2 |
| **Totals** | **4.1** | **93** | **.645** | **17** | **17** | **16** | **0** | **0** | **10** |

Pitching
L: Player 2-1
HBP: Player 2-13
Pitches-Strikes: Player 2-1 38-26, Player 2-12 20-11, Player 2-13 19-11, Player 2-14 19-13
Groundouts-Flyouts: Player 2-1 4-3, Player 2-12 0-2, Player 2-13 0-1, Player 2-14 1-2
First pitch strikes-Batters faced: Player 2-1 13-14, Player 2-12 3-8, Player 2-13 2-6, Player 2-14 3-6

### Clutch more stats

| Pitching | IP | #P | S% | H | R | ER | SO | BB | HR |
|---|---|---|---|---|---|---|---|---|---|
| Ben R. | 5.0 | 76 | .658 | 5 | 5 | 3 | 3 | 2 | 0 |
| **Totals** | **5.0** | **76** | **.658** | **5** | **5** | **3** | **3** | **2** | **0** |

Pitching
W: Ben R.
WP: Ben R.
Pitches-Strikes: Ben R. 76-50
Groundouts-Flyouts: Ben R. 5-5
First pitch strikes-Batters faced: Ben R. 15-24

# Hard 90 Clutch 12U Blows Out 023 985 Louisiana Blues Thanks To Big Fourth Inning

Hard 90 Clutch 12U put up nine runs in the fourth on its way to a 17-5 victory over 023 985 Louisiana Blues on Wednesday. Hard 90 Clutch 12U's big bats in the inning were led by home runs by Jack S, Jordan W, Ryan T , and Jack and a single by Taylor S.

023 985 Louisiana Blues got on the board in the first inning when Player 2-11 grounded out, scoring one run.

Hard 90 Clutch 12U knotted the game up at two in the bottom of the first inning, when Jordan homered on the first pitch of the at bat, scoring two runs.

Hard 90 Clutch 12U pulled away for good with two runs in the second inning. In the second Scott B hit a solo homer and Ty M hit a solo homer.

Hard 90 Clutch 12U notched nine runs in the fourth inning. The offensive onslaught by Hard 90 Clutch 12U was led by Jack, Jordan, Taylor, Ryan T and Jack, all sending runners across the plate with RBIs in the inning.

Ben R earned the win for Hard 90 Clutch 12U. He went five innings, allowing five runs on five hits and striking out three.

Player 2-1 took the loss for 023 985 Louisiana Blues. He lasted two and a third innings, allowing six hits and six runs while walking zero.

Hard 90 Clutch 12U socked ten home runs on the day. Brady R had a long ball in the third and fifth innings. Jack went deep in the fourth and fourth innings. Jordan had a dinger in the first and fourth innings. Ryan had a homer in the fourth inning. Scott went yard in the second inning. Taylor went for the long ball in the third inning. Ty had a four bagger in the second inning.

Hard 90 Clutch 12U racked up 17 hits on the day. Scott, Jack, Jordan, Brady, and Taylor each had multiple hits for Hard 90 Clutch 12U. Jack and Scott each collected three hits to lead Hard 90 Clutch 12U.

Player 2-15 led 023 985 Louisiana Blues with two hits in three at bats.

# 12

## Cooperstown Day 7

Wake-up came early again in the barracks: 6:30. The sun was shining in Dreams Park and it was a beautiful day for a championship run.

As usual, the boys woke up, reflected on what they needed to do to be successful, made their beds and headed to the showers. They again opted for energy bars instead of breakfast before heading out to the cages to get Championship Day started.

The boys were in the final 16, set for an 8:30 a.m. date with the undefeated sixth seed Lake Elmo from Minnesota. Since the Clutch were the lower seed, the boys would be visitors wearing their blue jerseys.

As usual, Captain Jack started things with a bang, sending the first pitch of the game well over the center-field fence for a 1-0 lead. The rest of the inning was quiet for the Clutch.

Brady was on the hill. Lake Elmo was going to be a tough matchup, scoring twice in its half of the first to take a 2-1 lead.

After a scoreless second, the Clutch got going in the third. Ryan and Jack started the inning with singles before Jordan doubled off the right-field wall to drive in Ryan. Ben singled to drive in Jack and then Jordan scored on a wild pitch; it was 4-2, Clutch.

Brady held Lake Elmo at bay in the third and fourth. In the top of the fifth, the Clutch had runners on the corners with Ty up. Knowing that every run would matter in this elimination game, Coach Eric went to the bunt-and-run play. Taylor broke for second and Ty put down the perfect bunt between first and second for a hit, scoring Brady.

But Lake Elmo erupted for six runs in the bottom of the inning, grabbing an 8-5 lead.

And there it was, the Clutch's tournament life coming down to the last inning, needing to score three runs. Jack led off the inning with a hit-by-pitch, but two outs later, the Clutch was down to their last out. A routine popup to the pitcher was dropped and once again the Clutch had life.

Up stepped Brady with a chance to tie the game. He worked the count to 2-1 before he hit a tank over the center-field fence to tie the game 8-8.

Next up was Taylor. After working the count to 2-1, Taylor hit a no-doubter to give the Clutch the lead, 9-8. The Clutch was heading to the home half of the sixth needing three outs to advance.

Unfortunately, this was not to be the Clutch's day. Lake Elmo continued to put bat to ball and scored two runs to win the game 10-9 in a walkoff.

It was a tough end to a great tournament. The boys had put in a ton of work and it paid off with a 7-1 Cooperstown run. Coach Eric called the boys and families up for an emotional postgame meeting.

He told the boys how proud he was of each and every one of them. The Clutch boys had put in the work to prepare for this tournament and battled until the last out of the game. They never gave up, learned a ton of life lessons and had a lot of fun along the way.

While the loss stung, the value of team was quickly remembered. The boys headed up to the Cooperstown Dreams Park sign to commemorate the trip with some photos. The Clutch boys then headed out for some team bonding at the Cooperstown Fun Park and ice cream at Cooper's Barn.

The boys reported back to the Village at 4:00 p.m. for closing ceremonies, where each player was given a ring and inducted into the Youth Baseball Hall of Fame. Everyone was treated to a fireworks show before watching the championship game.

This was truly an amazing week with a special group of boys.

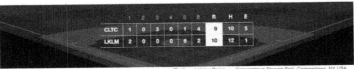

| | 1 | 2 | 3 | 4 | 5 | 6 | R | H | E |
|---|---|---|---|---|---|---|---|---|---|
| CLTC | 1 | 0 | 3 | 0 | 1 | 4 | 9 | 10 | 5 |
| LKLM | 2 | 0 | 0 | 0 | 6 | 2 | 10 | 12 | 1 |

**GameStream**     Final    League Game    Cooperstown Dreams Park, Cooperstown, NY, USA

## 9   Hard 90 Clutch 12U     Thursday, July 25   5:30AM     Lake Elmo 12AAA Travel 12U   10

### Clutch more stats

| Lineup | AB | R | H | RBI | BB | SO |
|---|---|---|---|---|---|---|
| Jack S. | 2 | 3 | 2 | 1 | 1 | 0 |
| Jordan W. | 3 | 1 | 1 | 1 | 0 | 2 |
| Ben R. | 4 | 0 | 1 | 1 | 0 | 0 |
| Carter G. | 4 | 1 | 0 | 0 | 0 | 2 |
| Brady R. | 3 | 2 | 1 | 3 | 1 | 2 |
| Taylor S. | 4 | 1 | 2 | 1 | 0 | 2 |
| Ty M. | 3 | 0 | 1 | 1 | 1 | 1 |
| Ian P. | 1 | 0 | 0 | 0 | 0 | 1 |
| Scott B. | 2 | 0 | 1 | 0 | 0 | 0 |
| Ryan T. | 2 | 1 | 1 | 0 | 0 | 0 |
| Eric L. | 1 | 0 | 0 | 0 | 0 | 1 |
| **Totals** | **29** | **9** | **10** | **8** | **3** | **11** |

**Batting**
2B: Jordan W.
HR: Brady R., Jack S., Taylor S.
TB: Scott B., Ty M., Ben R., Brady R. 4, Ryan T., Jack S. 5, Taylor S. 5, Jordan W. 2
RBI: Ty M., Ben R., Brady R. 3, Jack S., Taylor S., Jordan W.
ROE: Carter G.
FC: Scott B.
HBP: Jack S., Jordan W.
SB: Ben R.

Totals
Team QAB: 13 (38.24%)
Scott B. 2, Ty M. 2, Brady R. 2, Jack S. 3, Taylor S. 3, Jordan W.

Team LOB: 7

Fielding
E: Ty M. 2, Taylor S., Jordan W. 2
DP: Ty M., Jack S.

### Lake Elmo 12AAA Travel 12U more stats

| Lineup | AB | R | H | RBI | BB | SO |
|---|---|---|---|---|---|---|
| #1 | 3 | 1 | 1 | 0 | 0 | 0 |
| #3 | 2 | 2 | 1 | 0 | 1 | 0 |
| #4 | 3 | 0 | 1 | 0 | 0 | 0 |
| #14 | 2 | 0 | 0 | 0 | 1 | 0 |
| #12 | 3 | 1 | 3 | 1 | 0 | 0 |
| #2 | 3 | 1 | 0 | 0 | 0 | 0 |
| #13 | 2 | 1 | 1 | 0 | 0 | 0 |
| #11 | 3 | 1 | 0 | 0 | 0 | 1 |
| #10 | 3 | 0 | 2 | 2 | 0 | 1 |
| #15 | 2 | 1 | 0 | 1 | 0 | 0 |
| #9 | 2 | 1 | 2 | 1 | 0 | 0 |
| #8 | 2 | 1 | 1 | 3 | 0 | 0 |
| **Totals** | **30** | **10** | **12** | **8** | **3** | **2** |

**Batting**
2B: #12, #15
HR: #8
TB: #12 4, #4, #1, #13, #10 3, #3, #9 2, #8 4
RBI: #12, #10 2, #15, #8, #8 3
ROE: #4, #11, #2 2
FC: #14, #15
GIDP: #14, #8
SB: #2, #3

Totals
Team QAB: 13 (39.39%)
#12 3, #14 2, #4, #11, #13, #10, #3, #15, #9, #8

Team LOB: 5

Fielding
E: #13

### Clutch more stats

| Pitching | IP | #P | S% | H | R | ER | SO | BB | HR |
|---|---|---|---|---|---|---|---|---|---|
| Brady R. | 4.1 | 65 | .723 | 9 | 7 | 6 | 1 | 2 | 1 |
| Taylor S. | 0.2 | 18 | .778 | 1 | 1 | 0 | 0 | 0 | 0 |
| Carter G. | 0.1 | 16 | .750 | 2 | 2 | 1 | 1 | 1 | 0 |
| **Totals** | **5.1** | **99** | **.737** | **12** | **10** | **7** | **2** | **3** | **1** |

**Pitching**
L: Carter G.
WP: Taylor S.
Pitches-Strikes: Carter G. 16-12, Brady R. 65-47, Taylor S. 18-14
Groundouts-Flyouts: Carter G. 0-0, Brady R. 8-1, Taylor S. 1-0
First pitch strikes-Batters faced: Carter G. 4-5, Brady R. 19-24, Taylor S. 4-4

### Lake Elmo 12AAA Travel 12U more stats

| Pitching | IP | #P | S% | H | R | ER | SO | BB | HR |
|---|---|---|---|---|---|---|---|---|---|
| #12 | 4.0 | 69 | .638 | 6 | 4 | 4 | 7 | 2 | 1 |
| #3 | 0.2 | 24 | .667 | 2 | 1 | 1 | 1 | 1 | 0 |
| #13 | 1.0 | 23 | .696 | 2 | 4 | 0 | 2 | 0 | 2 |
| #10 | 0.1 | 6 | .500 | 0 | 0 | 0 | 1 | 0 | 0 |
| **Totals** | **6.0** | **122** | **.648** | **10** | **9** | **8** | **11** | **3** | **3** |

**Pitching**
W: #10
HBP: #12, #13
WP: #12, #3
Pitches-Strikes: #12 69-44, #13 23-16, #10 6-3, #3 24-16
Groundouts-Flyouts: #12 0-5, #13 1-0, #10 0-0, #3 0-0
First pitch strikes-Batters faced: #12 11-21, #13 5-7, #10 0-1, #3 3-5

# In Walk-Off, Hard 90 Clutch 12U Loses To Lake Elmo 12AAA Travel 12U

A walk-off left Hard 90 Clutch 12U on the wrong end of a 10-9 defeat to Lake Elmo 12AAA Travel 12U on Thursday. Lake Elmo 12AAA Travel 12U was down 9-8 in the bottom of the sixth inning when #10 doubled on a 0-1 count, scoring two runs.

Hard 90 Clutch 12U collected ten hits and Lake Elmo 12AAA Travel 12U had 12 in the high-scoring affair.

Lake Elmo 12AAA Travel 12U captured the lead in the first inning when #12 singled on the first pitch of the at bat, scoring one run.

Lake Elmo 12AAA Travel 12U scored six runs in the fifth inning. Lake Elmo 12AAA Travel 12U's big inning was driven by a single by #9, a home run by #8, a fielder's choice by #15, and an error on a ball put in play by #4.

#10 pitched Lake Elmo 12AAA Travel 12U to victory. He went one-third of an inning, allowing zero runs on zero hits, striking out one and walking zero. #13 and #3 entered the game out of the bullpen and helped to close out the game in relief.

Carter G took the loss for Hard 90 Clutch 12U. He lasted one-third of an inning, allowing two hits and two runs while striking out one and walking one.

Brady R started the game for Hard 90 Clutch 12U. He surrendered seven runs on nine hits over four and a third innings, striking out one #12 started the game for Lake Elmo 12AAA Travel 12U. He went four innings, allowing four runs on six hits and striking out seven

Hard 90 Clutch 12U hit three home runs on the day. Brady went deep in the sixth inning. Jack S went for the long ball in the first inning. Taylor S had a long ball in the sixth inning.

Hard 90 Clutch 12U tallied ten hits on the day. Jack and Taylor all had multiple hits for Hard 90 Clutch 12U. Taylor and Jack all had two hits to lead Hard 90 Clutch 12U.

Lake Elmo 12AAA Travel 12U tallied 12 hits. #12, #9, and #10 each managed multiple hits for Lake Elmo 12AAA Travel 12U. #12 led Lake Elmo 12AAA Travel 12U with three hits in three at bats.

# 13

## Summary

The Hard 90 Clutch had an amazing run in Coopertown. Eleven good friends became brothers over a weeklong summer baseball camp.

The Clutch trained together for more than three years with the goal of winning the Cooperstown Dreams Park tournament. The team battled together against teams from all over North America, posted a 7-1 record, hit 46 home runs, and came from behind to win twice against nationally ranked teams, all while respecting the game of baseball. Even though they came up short on their goal of winning the championship, the boys gained a ton throughout the process.

They learned the value of doing their best over a period of time. The personal growth each player experienced over the three years was tremendous and prepared them for their next quest of playing high school baseball.

They learned the value of a team—how fun it could be to work with each other to accomplish a goal. Through that work they would become brothers, part of a special fraternity of ballplayers.

The boys learned that to be successful, you had to overcome adversity; many times during the tournament and the season they found themselves down and worked together to be victorious.

They also learned that if you continually learn, you can never lose.

# ABOUT HARD 90 BASEBALL

Hard 90 Baseball is a training facility in El Dorado Hills, California. Hard 90 Baseball has been sending teams to Cooperstown since 2006, winning the Cooperstown Dreams Park tournament twice.

Hard 90 offers classes and private lessons for hitting, pitching, and fielding. In addition to training, Hard 90 fields travel baseball teams for ages nine to 18. Since its establishment in 2005, over 300 Hard 90 alumni have gone on to play college and professional baseball. www.hard90baseball.com

# ABOUT THE AUTHOR

Eric Walczykowski is a husband, father, baseball coach, and corporate executive. Through the years, Eric has had the opportunity to serve technology and life-science companies as CEO, division president, venture capitalist, board member, and advisor.

Since 2014, Eric and his wife Colleen have owned Hard 90 Baseball in El Dorado Hills, California. Eric is a strong believer that sports are one of the greatest opportunities to teach kids about life.

Eric is the author of *The Hard 90 Mindset*, a book that helps athletes reach their full potential on and off the baseball field.

Made in the USA
Monee, IL
14 March 2021